How to
Sell More Tickets
To Your Show

Other Resources by Brian Teasley

"How to Market & Sell Your CREATEPACE Book"

Available via CreateSpace.com & Amazon.com

"How to Improve Your Marketing" – A series of free articles for businesses

Available at: www.teasley.net/free_stuff.htm

How to
Sell More Tickets
To Your Show

By

BRIAN TEASLEY

For additional information & copies: www.teasley.net

"Remember, we are all just holding pens."

-Brian Teasley

CONTENTS

CONTENTS (continued)

WARM UP ACT

I'm going to help you **sell tickets to your shows**.

You might be an up-and-coming producer trying to make your mark with some smaller up-and-coming shows. You might be an actor trying to promote your solo show, or your company's show. You might be the head of an acting company, or a venue owner.

Regardless, I'm going to help you **sell tickets to your shows**.

New York City, where this book was written, is full of amazing actors and performers of all types. They come here from all over the world to "make it". I have met some amazingly talented performers. Some of them have become famous since I have met them. Some already were. Some soon will be. But virtually none of them know how to market themselves. None of them know how to sell tickets to their own shows. That's where I come in.

I have always had an interest in performances, shows, and music. I have put on sold out shows here in New York City. I have met some of the top producers on Broadway. I have been in on discussions regarding major, medium and small shows here. But those are only some of the reasons why I am able to help you sell tickets to your shows.

I can help you sell tickets to your shows because I have spent over fifteen years "behind the scenes" at major "Madison Avenue" type ad agencies, working with some of the most famous brands in the world. I've worked on projects for, and been at the corporate headquarters of AT&T, FedEx, American Express, USAToday, and a very large number of other companies.

I have helped them with data, technology and testing of "creative" pieces. I have helped them test offers to see which ones garner the most response from customers. I have helped them test emails campaigns, direct mail campaigns, newspaper ads, etc…

And guess what…. Many of the techniques and processes used by these major advertising agencies apply to the selling of YOUR show. And in this day and age with computers and technology being the way they are there is no reason you can't conduct a marketing campaign on par with, if not MORE effective for your show than that of a major advertising agency.

I am going to share with you inside "secrets" – that really aren't that secret. I am going to share with you the methods they would use to sell a show – and some they wouldn't use because most ad agencies are focused on "major" clients and want to execute "major" ad campaigns.

The ad agencies would also never take on your show as a client. Or rather, you wouldn't want to pay the fees they would charge you for doing the things that – with this book – you are going to know how to do for yourself. Any ad agency will take you on as a client if you pay them. So if you have a ton of money to spare and want to get mediocre results for a lot of your money – hire an ad agency.   If you don't have a ton of money to spare, read on.

Who This Book is For

First let's get a few things out of the way.

Marketing a show and selling tickets to it takes work.   It also requires that the show is good. If you have a good show and are willing to do the work it takes to sell tickets to it, then read on. If you are doing a lame show or a show with a very limited audience, then don't bother to reading this book. Selling tickets to a show requires "word of mouth" advertising (more on that to come later, including how to get it*).   *If your show is poor or there is no real audience for it, you are not going to generate any word-of-mouth advertising and sales. Because of this, you should spend your time doing anything else other than trying to market your show – because there isn't a large ticket-buying audience for it.*

There are certainly times when this is ok. You might have a simple show that might be of interest to "friends and family" and that's about it. It's good experience for those involved, it's a fun and/or interesting event for those that attend, and everybody attending gets a nice credit on their life resume and has a good time. If that's what you have, that's great. Realize it, and don't spend the time trying to sell many tickets to it.

But if that is the type of show you are doing, then there is no reason to read this book and put in all the effort involved in marketing and selling tickets to your show. On the other hand, if you do have a good show and you know there is an audience out there for it, read on.

Marketing, Sales, PR, Advertising

Just what is "marketing", "publicity", "PR", "Advertising", and "Sales"? Aren't they the same thing?

On this topic, let me first say this: If you are a little confused as to what the difference is between these things – or don't know exactly what the function is of these different areas, don't worry. The ad agencies actually like it that way, because it makes them more important to you. BUT, I'm going to explain it to you.

Most major companies have a marketing department. In the case of your show, most likely YOU are the marketing department. The marketing "department" (that's you) is in charge of "all of the above" – at least from a focal standpoint. The marketing department coordinates all of the above activities.

Now the marketing department at a major company doesn't necessarily DO all of the above things. They will subcontract them out to various entities. They hire one company to do their public relations and publicity work, another company to design their advertising and get it placed in the correct locations (television, radio, etc). The ad agency, in turn might hire a media buying company – and the media buyers actually negotiate the "buying" of ad space and make the purchase.

They might also subcontract out the development of the logo, artwork, etc.. to a "creative" person (e.g. graphic designer). The ad agencies do NOT want you to know these things (more on that later – and why it is a great thing that you now know these secrets), but now you do.

Major companies separately have a "sales" department. The people in this department are the people who actually sell the product to the customers. Their customers might be major department stores (think lines of clothing sold to stores) – or end consumers (salesmen on the floor of the department store selling you clothes to wear to your opening night).

As the marketing department for your show, you are going to be a lot more involved and "hands on" in all these activities (marketing, PR, sales) than the marketing department for a major company. You still might "sub out" some of these tasks to 3rd parties, but since you end goal is to SELL TICKETS, you are going to want to be heavily involved in every step of the process – and with all of these activities.

Ad agencies OFTEN do not care about sales. They'll claim they are only concerned about "building your brand image" and "awareness". That's because if the tickets don't sell, they can say it wasn't their fault. In their defense, if you show stinks, it isn't going to sell tickets once the word gets out... so in some since it won't be the agency's fault.

If you are going to be involved in these activities - and you need to execute in ALL of these areas to be successful - then you need to know the differences between them.

Marketing is comprised of all of the activities that get the word out about your show. It's everything just short of the actual selling of the tickets. So publicity, public relations, "guerilla marketing" (e.g. "street teams") , advertising and anything else that gets the word out about your show is ALL marketing.

Publicity, Public Relations, "PR"

As mentioned above, an ad agency hired by a major marketing department might sub contract the "PR" work to a publicity agent or "PR Firm". It is the job of the PR firm or publicity agent to get coverage of your product/show. This coverage is usually in the form of coverage in print (newspapers, magazines), or other media (radio, television, or online).

You are going to do your own publicity work

Advertising

In general advertising is paying to get the word out about your show. Obviously, if you purchase an advertisement in a newspaper or magazine then you are advertising. Putting up signs or buying space on a billboard is "outdoor" advertising. Sending out a postcard to 1,000 specially selected people is considered "direct marketing", rather than advertising. This is because you are directly targeting specific people, rather than "carpet bombing" the airwaves with an advertisement about your show.

Many people consider "advertising" very expensive for what it returns in terms of sales. It is also often quite costly.

I'm going to show you how to do your own marketing and advertising – AND how to reduce the cost of any "expensive" advertising should you decide to execute some of the more expensive options.

Sales

This is the actual act of selling tickets. It has to happen somehow – and there are choices to be made (online sales, phone sales, box office sales, etc.).

Marketing

Marketing your show requires all of the above activities, plus some things that do not fit neatly into any of the above categories. The process starts with a very solid understanding of your show and who the target audience is. It continues through the development of marketing materials - including the show's logo, color scheme, press kits, website(s), sales material, ads, postcards, etc..

Some people might say marketing ends when somebody steps up to purchase a ticket (or hopefully many tickets!) to your show. Guess what? They are VERY wrong. More on that later.

If you really want to be successful, your marketing efforts will include activities and interaction with graphic designers, actors, concession stand sales people, people on the street, people online, web site designers, box office staff, street teams, and many others.

It takes a lot of work and a lot of coordinated effort to successfully market a show. If you have a ton of money, the easiest way is to hire an agency and let them do it for you. But that will cost you a lot of money. That was your last warning. If you prefer to do it yourself (or don't have a choice, due to monetary considerations) read on.

The coordination of your efforts is going to be aided by your *"Marketing Plan"*. That is simply a list of all the activities you are going to do and a schedule of when you are going to do them.

However, prior to developing your plan you have to fully understand your show from a marketing standpoint. Even if you wrote the show yourself, I promise that you do not fully understand it from a marketing standpoint.

That's what we are going to take care of next.

Understanding Your Show

Understanding Your Show

Who is going to come to your show, and why?

Those are the first two questions you have to answer to develop your marketing plan. **DO NOT skip this section** of this book. It drives everything else in your marketing efforts. Once you develop your "target market" and your show's "positioning" (explained later) then you will be on your way to knowing where to advertise, seek publicity, what "angles" to use, etc..

You might think it's easy to answer those questions. **It's not.** If you take the quick and easy answers, then you don't have the right answers. Read through the rest of this and do the required thinking – then you'll have what you need to market your show.

A first pass at answering the above questions might take one to two hours of discussion with yourself and anyone else you think is appropriate and helpful. You'll inevitably re-visit the questions again later, but the harder you think and the more carefully you answer these questions, the more successful your marketing efforts will be.

The **"target market"** the advertising big-wigs like to talk about is the center core of your audience. "Everybody will like my show, so that is my target audience", is not an acceptable or useful answer.

Different shows appeal to different people, and for different reasons. The target audience for a punk rock show might be "College kids with an anti-establishment attitude". "Nostalgic 50 year old women" might be the target audience for a revival of "South Pacific".

You really, really need to think about who is going to be attracted to your show – and why they are going to come. What is going to convince them that they should skip an evening with their television set, or books, instant messaging, or whatever it is they usually do during their evening, and come see your show?

It's very possible that your target audience will be comprised of a couple of different types of people. They will have different reasons for coming to your show. However, it's very difficult to sell to multiple groups of people with a small advertisement, postcard, or 60 second radio spot. So you must decide the top (largest and/or most influential) group or two, and that is your target audience.

Of course, that doesn't mean other people can't or won't come to your show. But if you are spending time, effort and money trying to attract an audience you want to go after those people that are most likely to come to your show.

Most people involved with shows do not think this through far enough, if they think it through at all. Let me share a story with you that occurred inside a major ad agency. It proves that not even the "Madison Avenue" types always do what they should do.

I was sitting in the New York office of the President of a major ad agency. I was with the President of the company and the head "creative director". This guy ran the "creative" aspect of their campaigns, including strategy, concepts, and artistic design. He also happened to be from England – where soccer is a major sport.

The task was to come up with a new concept for a large American fast food joint. This particular fast food company is very popular in the African American community, which is their target market. The "brilliant idea" that I heard from the creative director was to tie the restaurant in with the World Cup soccer tournament. The "tag line" was going to be something along the lines of "The Whole World is Going Crazy" for the restaurant.

How well would this approach resonate with the target market for the restaurant? Well, the World Cup and soccer are not major events in the United States. And in the African American communities, soccer is even less of a draw. So the plan I heard from a major ad agency was to market this restaurant to the target market using a message that had absolutely NO relevancy to it.

You can not afford to make the same mistake.

So let's take some time to think about your show, what it is about, and who will like it and why.

What is your show about?

You are going to be asked this question many, many times during the process of marketing and selling tickets to your show. You need to be able to "nail" this answer. Because the work you do on the answer to this question, right now, will come in infinitely handy when you are on the David Letterman show (or more likely a local television or radio show, but you never know) and he says to you, "Tell me a little bit about your show."

To me at least, this is a surprisingly difficult question to answer. Please notice the question above is not "What happens in your show?" The question is "What is your show about?"

If someone asks "What is Romeo and Juliet about?" the answer is not something like:

Bad:

"It's about a guy and a girl who meet at a party. The guy decides he wants to see more of her despite the fact that his family does not get along with hers. They meet secretly and vow their love to each other. Then the guy gets into a fight and kills the girl's brother. Despite this, her love for him continues and the run away together. Because of a series of misunderstandings they both commit suicide."

Better:

Romeo and Juliet is about romantic love and human prejudice. It's about a poignant love and is story for the ages. It is a story that was written in the 1700's but is still applicable today.

It's about two young lovers whose families hold an "ancient grudge" against each other. Because of this, they are forbidden to see each other. Yet their love transcends – and ends up being the cause of their demise.

The "bad" description above is more of a plot summary. The "good" description gets to the heart of the matter of the show.

As for your show, you might have a few opinions about what the show is about – but you need to spend time thinking about it so you know what is at the core of your show.

Let's work on the description of "Romeo and Juliet" a bit more.

If I was trying to sell tickets to it I would first come up with different descriptions to use depending on who I was talking to. For an older target demographic, I would mention that it is a Shakespeare play. If I'm talking to teenage boys, there is no chance they want to see a Shakespeare play. They DO want to see a gorgeous teen girl and a guy who hook up despite their parents not wanting them to do so. (See "Spring Awakening" - www.springawakening.com)

But let's ignore the Shakespeare factor and look at a couple of possible descriptions:

Version 1:

"Romeo and Juliet" is a dramatic, touching, and entertaining play about love. Set in renaissance era Italy (unless it's the movie version, in which case it's modern day East Los Angeles) two teenagers become lovers despite their families forbidding them to see each other. What happens to them is the "two hours traffic of (the) stage".

Now let's note that in the fourteen line prologue to the story, Shakespeare does his own plot summary and tells us what the story is about. It's really about the "fearful passage of their death-mark'd love". That is a much more powerful statement about the show than simply saying it's a "play about love". With this in mind, maybe we should change our statement about what the show is about to:

Version 2:

"Romeo and Juliet" is a dramatic, touching, and entertaining play about the fearful passage of a death marked love.

So which show do you want to see, the one described in Version 1 or the one described in Version 2? Despite the fact that version 1 is a bit longer and tells a little bit more about the plot, but Version 2 is MUCH more enticing. Version 1 is ok. It does tell what the story about – but Version 2 is a lot more "short and sweet" - if you can call "fearful passage" and "death marked love" sweet!

Short and sweet is much more powerful, much more useful, and MUCH more likely to sell tickets to your show.

Get It Down on Paper

I showed you version 1 and version 2 above to illustrate the iterative nature of developing your knowledge about what the show is about. You need to refine and refine your description of what your show is about until it reaches the point where you say "Wow. Ok, THAT's what our show is about". You'll know when you have reached that point because you will feel comfortable with the end result.

Again, this process takes more than 15 minutes to complete.

Notice in both versions of the "Romeo and Juliet" description I snuck in a couple of words specifically about the type of show it is. "Dramatic" and "touching" are both descriptive words (which actually get a bit to the "benefits" of the show – more later) and "play" tells the prospective ticket buyer that it's a play. It's not a musical. It's not a documentary. It's not a concert. It's a play.

So what is your show? Is it:

- A Romantic/Comedy (which is what many, movies are described as being)
- A Broadway-type Musical
- A Punk Rock Showcase of 5 local, state, national, contest-winning bands?
- A thought provoking drama
- A heart wrenching drama?

- A touching, comedic one woman play
- A play that takes a controversial look at…

The more accurate and descriptive words you can easily and quickly use in your description, the better. "It's a love story" will attract a few people. "It's a love story about the fearful passage of a death marked love" will attract the same first few people PLUS more.

And what is your show about? Is it…

- About a girl "finding herself"? (E.g. Perhaps the "Wizard of Oz" – finding that her love at home ("There's no place like home…") is what's most important, despite the fantastical journeys)
- About "teenage awakening" ("Spring Awakening")?
- "Fearful passage of their death-marked love"?

You could say that "Romeo and Juliet" is about love. You could say it's about a "death-marked love". But the play is really about how the love starts, grows, and ultimately ends. It's about the *passage* of their love. And in part it is a fearful passage. Shakespeare was a pretty good copywriter.

So what is your show about?

Positioning

"Positioning" of your show is very important. Where/what is your show in comparison to others? It is summed up in a "positioning statement" that tells your prospective audience members about your show and how it differs from other shows.

The good news is you have control over your positioning statement.

A positioning statement for "South Pacific" might be:

To 60 year olds, South Pacific is a deeply moving drama about racism during World War II with extraordinary music the way it they wish it still was.

Rent was once positioned as:

The musical for people who hate musicals

Spring Awakening's positioning statement, taken from their website is:

The groundbreaking fusion of morality, sexuality, and rock and roll that has awakened Broadway like no other musical in years.

Notice that all these statements tell you what type of show it is (musical, in all cases). They also point a little bit to the target audience. "They way they wish (music) still was" points to an older nostalgic audience, while "...sexuality and rock and roll" points to a younger audience. Spring Awakening has a line of younger people waiting for less expensive "rush" tickets every day. South Pacific definitely attracts an older crowd.

Note: If you are near a computer, go to the Spring Awakening web site and find their "The Story" page. It has this positioning statement, plus a description of what the story is about. It is exactly what we are talking about in our discussion here – and you can see the results they achieved using a "High Powered" ad agency and lots of money. You can achieve the same results with a pen, paper and a couple of hours of thinking.

The "what's it about" and positioning we are talking about in this book are exactly what was behind the discussions that occurred at the ad agency with the producers of Spring Awakening. I can hear the discussions in my head. Through lots of "word-smithing", the sentence "Well, it's about these kids in school (oh and by the way it's Germany in the late 1800's) who struggle with issues involving sex, rape, homosexuality and piano lessons…" was eventually distilled to "The groundbreaking fusion of morality…" etc..

Those discussions cost tens of thousands of dollars in fees. But – YOU know what your show is about better than anyone else. So you can follow the examples and ideas presented here and determine the perfect positioning statement for YOUR show. All it will cost you is time and concentrated thought. And you can send me any portion of the tens of thousands in fees I just saved you.

But the positioning statement is very important. It gives the distilled essence of your show – and is a driving force behind all of your marketing efforts. Every aspect of what you do to market your show and sell tickets to it stems in some way from the description of the show ("What's it about?") – and your positioning statement.

Your Target Market

Who Will Come to Your Show – And WHY?

Before we got into what your show is really about, we talked about your "target market". Now that you know exactly what your show is about – and have developed your positioning statement, it should be a little clearer to you who is actually the appropriate target market for your show. Who is most likely to come see it and enjoy it?

In the case of a show that talks about sex and rock and roll… you've narrowed the "everybody will like it" towards a younger crowd. AND it's obvious that this show should appeal to men. So maybe the appropriate target market is 16 to 30 year olds, including both men and women.

Can we narrow it down any further? If the music was "hip-hop" would that change the demographics of who might come to the show? Certainly. When "Raisin in the Sun" was on Broadway, it featured Sean Puffy P-Diddy Combs – or whatever the heck his name is at the moment. The audience had a lot more black people in it than a normal Broadway show. So if you were ever going to "target market" a black audience, it would be on a show that would appeal to them.

You need to figure out *exactly* who is in your target market.

Once you know who is in your target market, write down everything you know about them. What do they do on a daily/weekly basis? Where do they shop? What do they read? Do they eat out? Where? When? Some types of people hang out at fancy restaurants. Other's only go out in the summer to the Friday Family Fish fry. Do they spend time online? What sites?

You need to know what they do because the WHERE portion tells you where you must be with your marketing messages/efforts to reach them. The WHAT are they doing informs you what your options might be and/or what is the appropriate vehicle for your marketing.

For example, if they go to the Friday Fish Fry maybe you can convince the owner of the joint to let you put up table top displays/postcards on each table. Maybe you entice him to do so by offering a free ticket to raffle off... or a portion of sales bought from him go to charity... or to him if he'll keep a stack of tickets on hand and sell them and keep the cards on display for the run of your show. He's a businessman; he wants income – so give him a cut. And/or maybe your advertisements/emails/posts says "Purchase tickets at Hal's Restaurant".

If he runs a 24-hour diner and he agrees to sell tickets for you, in effect you were just able to hire someone to staff a box office for you for 24 hours per day – at no cost to you. This might be more beneficial than you first know.

On the other hand, if your audience is more likely to be in some posh restaurant in the area of your theater, then maybe you are lucky enough to be doing a musical and your piano player can do a few songs with your lead singer... and you can do a set of songs and include some from the shows. Make darn sure you have cards from the show, a place to take people's emails, cds to sell or hand out, etc....

But we are getting way ahead of ourselves. Those are a couple of the fun things you can do. I wanted to give you a quick understanding of how knowing your target market impacts your marketing efforts.

We are still in the creative, laying-the-ground-floor development portion or our marketing efforts, so let's get back to that. Now that you know what your show is about, and who your target market is, you need to know WHY your audience will come to your show. What will they get out of it? What is the benefit to them of their attending?

Benefits

Benefits are the things the audience receives from attending your show. Possible benefits to coming to your show include things like:

- Laugh so hard your eyes will water
- Learn about an era from the past
- Challenge your thoughts about (insert topic here)
- Be deeply moved by...
- Get scared out of your wits
- Hear the coolest music since...
- Be the first to hear/see the new show from...
- Meet industry folks to further your career

- Meet other people with fantastic/cool taste like yours
- Help the local actors (or "your friends") further their career

Notice that the last three are a bit different from the rest. They don't really have anything to do with the content of your show itself, but they do have to do with how some people may benefit from your show. You need to be aware of these benefits and play them up when the time is right. I certainly know of shows where some audience members are there mostly in hopes of furthering their careers. There's nothing wrong with that at all... and you might be able to figure out a way to tap into those people to assist in your marketing efforts.

So since at this point you know what your show is about and who is in your target audience, the next step is to figure out what benefits your target audience members receive from attending your show. There may be a few, but you are going to have to narrow it down to your top one or two to focus on in your marketing efforts.

For "Spring Awakening" they went with things like "celebrate an unforgettable journey"... after which "Broadway may never be the same again". So there is a celebration of sorts as a benefit, and I'm going to witness something that may change Broadway forever – so I get the benefit of seeing something new AND being there "when it happened". That all sounds good to me.

Interestingly, one of the groundbreaking aspects of "Spring Awakening" is the excellent way they've used the internet to promote the show. They came out immediately with online videos, ring tones, wallpapers and more... all appealing (correctly) to their younger target audience members. So even the marketing of the show may change Broadway forever.

That's just one example. You have to spend some serious thinking time coming up with the actual benefits people will receive if they come to your show. "They'll have a good time" or "They'll be entertained" probably isn't the best answer. "You'll be entertained by fantastic new you'll-be-humming-them-the-next-day never been heard before electro-pop songs sung by (insert your town's name here)'s best electro-pop singers" is a bit better. It won't fit on a postcard, but it's better.

If you think you have distinctly different groups who will come to your show, *you have to understand the benefits for each of them.*

The reason, if it's not obvious, is that when you communicate with your prospective audience members you are going to tell them what the show is about and what the benefits to them are going to be when they come. When you talk to different target groups, you can mention the specific benefits they will be interested in.

Unique Selling Proposition

Some ad people like to talk about a product's or show's "Unique Selling Proposition" or "USP". This is the thing that makes your show unique. It's **the reason somebody should come to your show** instead of any other show they could attend.

A great example of a unique selling proposition was, until lawyers got involved, Domino Pizza's "30 Minutes or Free" selling proposition. They didn't even ever say the pizza was good. They just said you'd receive it in 30 minutes or it would be free. It was a wildly successful USP.

If Julia Roberts is in your show, you have an easy to find USP. If you win an award, or a cast member has won an award, or if your show has a scene in which somebody juggles flaming cats, then you can think about using those as unique selling propositions. If there are costumed cats on stage for hours, or a real helicopter in your show, or if the police shut you down last time – you might have a unique selling proposition to work with.

Imagine an ad reading, "Tickets on Sale Now for 'Dogs' – the New Musical featuring Flaming Cat Juggling!" You will certainly get attention with marketing like that, as well as a visit from the People for the Ethical Treatment of Animals. That will get you some publicity, and you can figure out a way to make it beneficial.

You can read the rest of this book before developing the description and the positioning statement regarding your show, *but you can not execute anything discussed in the rest of this book without those items.* You need to know what benefits the show brings to your audience, because that will be the basis for the content in most of your tangible marketing efforts.

And if you can nail down a unique selling proposition, then you have developed a way to stand out above your competition. So strive to come up with a USP for your show. It might come in handy.

You must develop this understanding of your show and get it down on paper *before* you can start to sell tickets to your show.

Marketing Materials

Now that you have a solid understanding of what your show is about and how you want to position it, you can begin to develop your marketing materials. Everything you do, whether it's a postcard, a poster, a website, stationary for your show (you should have some!), a video, or any other piece of marketing collateral, needs to be coordinated in terms of "look and feel".

You want to develop a "brand" which runs throughout all of your marketing material, as well as through the show itself. I always think about "branding" like it's a red-hot brand that you are "branding" something with, just like cowboys do with cattle. Often branding something for your show is as simple as affixing your show's logo to it (e.g. t-shirt, postcard, mug). Branding actually goes much further than that. More on the total "brand experience" in a bit. First we'll discuss colors, fonts and logos.

However, let me insert a quick warning here: There is a huge tendency in marketing departments (especially when they are pushed by ad agencies) to get carried away with "branding" advertising. "Brand Advertising", by itself, **will not** sell tickets to your show.

I'd love to challenge any ad agency to put up a huge billboard in Times Square for me. The sign would be a "brand advertising" type sign about a show I'd be putting on. We'd do no other advertising. If the show sells out, I pay for the ad. Otherwise they eat the (substantial) costs. If there are any takers for this challenge, please get in touch with me.

So sure, do some thinking about the logo, etc., for your show. But these things are means to an end – which is selling tickets. They will not sell any tickets for you on their own. If you are going to spend an extra 2 hours designing a "new and better logo" – or an extra two hours creating a new press release and getting it out to the media, go with the press release efforts.

Colors, Fonts, logos

How do you decide what you should have as a logo for your show – and should you even have one? Inevitably people get really excited about developing their logo. It's a very visible part of marketing, and people to think at that is necessary to market a show is to develop a good, "creative" (whatever that means) logo.

Your logo needs to do a couple things – most importantly it needs to *help you sell tickets to your show*. The cutest, most creative logo in the world is worthless if it doesn't help you sell tickets to your show.

Secondly, it should help to convey what your show is about. Now you understand why we put in the time to understand our show and develop a positioning statement. The color scheme, fonts, and logos for a show should support your show by reflecting what it is about and where it is positioned.

The stenciled, "painted" logo for "Rent" (find it online if you don't know it already) does two things. It tells you the name of the show (which is helpful for buying tickets) and it reflects the "trying to get by", struggling life in the east village of New York City aspect of the show. If you get people wandering around with that logo on the front of their t-shirts – people are going to know the name of your show and at least subconsciously have an idea of what the show is about.

The logo for "Spring Awakening" consists of the words "SPRING AWAKENING" in black, sort of stenciled or run over with a paint roller, onto a rich dark red rectangle of red paint, but the rectangle is not quite complete because they ran out of paint when they were using the roller... or something like that.

The black contrasting with the red might allude to the edginess or rock and roll... but it certainly does not fit in with flowers coming up in the springtime, which you might misconstrue the story to be about if you just went by the title. So the logo says, "No you sexually activating teens – do not be alarmed. This show is NOT about daffodils and gentle April rain showers. It's actually about..." ...and then it doesn't tell you what the show is about. HOWEVER if you saw the photo that usually accompanied the logo, the iconic "guy with girl" photo, it clued you in big time as to what the show might actually be about.

The ad agency that put together the campaign for Spring Awakening obviously decided to go with black and red, which combined are strong, powerful colors. "SPRING AWAKENING" is all capitalized, which is also strong.

In contrast to this "South Pacific" is currently running at Lincoln Center in New York with a simply cursive script chosen for the words "South Pacific". That's all there is to the "logo". The elegance of the formal font lends itself to the "classiness" of the show. It is certainly a timeless classic that plays to a more formal audience than the rock and roll-ish target audience of "Spring Awakening".

So the colors, fonts, and logo you choose should all support your show – in the manner of the examples given. To look as professional as possible make all your marketing materials as consistent as possible. Notice the Spring Awakening website is heavily done in black and red. The background on all the pages is black, and red is splashed strategically around the page to give it an edgy look. ALL of your marketing materials should follow this pattern and be consistent.

How to Create Your Color Scheme and Logos

If you are like me, you are not talented enough to develop your own logo. I might have some ideas, but I'm not going to be able to come up with the finished product. You need a "creative" person (that's what ad agencies literally call them). That person might call themselves a "Graphic designer".

Hopefully you already know a few people like this. Otherwise, hit up craigslist and post to find somebody to help you develop a logo and a color scheme. It should not cost too much.

The good news is you might actually be able to get someone who works at a major ad agency to do the work for you. They'll charge you, but they will NOT charge you what it would cost if you had the ad agency do it for you. SAME end result, but much more affordable.

And who knows, maybe they'll do it for a few complimentary tickets or some type of barter deal. Remember, you have a cool product that people are going to pay money to see – so you have something of value with which to work. Plus "creative" types like working on creative, interesting projects. Trust me, they loathe working for major companies, except for the fact that it pays well.

To help the "creative" person, you might send them a **creative brief**. It might be a page or two of information. It contains a description of what the show is about, the positioning statement, the target market and a few other items that will help the "creative" person complete the project for which the brief is created. An example is below.

A creative brief also says what the objective of the project is (develop a color scheme? Logo?) and where and how the logo, etc., will be used. This is important, for example, as you have to consider what your logo will look like in a black and white print advertisement if you are going to run b/w print ads. Will it work on t-shirts? Is it read-able? Etc.

Creative Brief
Logo & "Look and Fell" Project for "Sublet"
03/04/09

Overview:
The show "Sublet" is scheduled to run September '09 through January 4th, 2010. It is a production of Brian Teasley and is scheduled to run at the Majestic Theater in New York City. For more information about Brian Teasley, please visit: www.teasley.net

Deliverable:
The deliverables for this project include a logo for the show, delivered in Photoshop .psd file format. The project also requires a color and font scheme to be delivered for use in all marketing materials. (Via .psd files or .doc or .ppt files). Exact color codes would be helpful if available.

Show Description:
The show is a musical spoof of the long running show "Rent". Instead of the cast celebrating life and dealing with adversity, this show wallows in the hardships and exaggerates them for comic effect. It is a satirical look at today's pop culture, with songs exaggerating how difficult people's lives our while they live in the richest country in the world. It starts out "Brady Bunch" but quickly degenerates into a combination of Jonathon Swift colored by Jerry Springer.

For the "Grew up with the Internet" set, it's a laugh-out-loud, funny, bitingly satirical rock and roll musical that skewers the pop culture that is force fed to them.

Primary Audience:
The show will resonate with a younger-than-usual Broadway crowd, maybe 18 to 35 year olds. Both male and female. Maybe above average education. For the initial run they will all be in the New York City area. We will first target the "local" audience, and then expand to the tourist audience.

The show plays a bit more to the cynical, perhaps those that feel they are "above" US and People magazine. There is some fairly hard rock and roll music in it. They are quite familiar with the online world, youtube, facebook, etc..

Look/Feel:
Whatever "Fun" feels like to an 18-40 year old crowd. This is not a "serious" show. It is more an escape from the barrage of television. It's "light" and "happy" overall, but cynical on the way to it's arrival there.

Show Benefits to Target Audience(s):
A chance to laugh at the ridiculousness of the "Hollywood (and other) Elite"
A refreshing yet cynical escape from today's pop culture.
Cutting Edge Music You Can Crank Up Loudly in Your Car
Not "boring" like other Broadway musicals for older audiences

Use:
It is expected that the logo and color scheme will be used in a variety of marketing materials, including t-shirts, postcards,

and print ads. Some black and white advertising IS possible, so this must be considered.

Timeline:
Logo, color scheme, "look and feel" needed by end of day - 3/20

Contact:
Brian Teasley (646-414-1100) or bteasley@teasley.net

A creative brief document to develop a logo is a little bit simpler than a creative brief for creating an advertisement. An ad will usually contain more information. So for the development of a logo and color scheme you can keep it fairly simple.

Ask your graphic designer to give you a few ideas/examples if possible. They might come back a few days later with some sketches or digital examples. You'll probably have some ideas for slight changes. If you have hired the person, they'll usually accept one round of changes at no charge. If you keep making changes you'll be using more of their time, so expect to compensate them for the extra work.

Finally, take a look at the logo for an upcoming show (which might be out by the time you are reading this) at: myspace.com/superchixrocks . It does a few things really well. Between the logo and the name of the show you know it's got something to do with rock and roll and women. The colors are certainly energetic, which is in line with the show.

I do have concerns about the logo (which looks great online on a digital screen) when it comes to transferring to print. I'm not sure the purple glow effect around the guitar will transfer to the offline world.

But that potential problem is not going to matter. The show is killer – and that's MUCH more important than the logo. Spend more time worrying about your show than on the logo. The "Show Experience" is where the word of mouth advertising is going to come from. It's not going to happen from the logo. The logo is really meant to attract someone's attention and remind someone about the show. Then they think, "Oh yeah, that's the show that Steve was telling us about... we should go see it!".

That's how marketing helps you sell tickets to your show.

More Marketing Materials

Some marketers like to talk about "Market, Message, and Medium" when they talk about marketing. The Market is the "target market" or group of people you want to hit with your message. Your message is what your show is about (description) and why they should see it (benefits, USP). The Medium is the "physical" way you are going to deliver your message – e.g. by television, radio, internet (website, email, banner ads, youtube video).

Where you are going to market your show and with type of material is determined by your target audience and your budget. I'm going to assume you do not have enough money for a major television buy or a major outdoor ad campaign. (An ad sign for your show in the New York City subway, in 1/10th of the subway cars, costs approximately $20,000 for one month).

The good news is TV probably isn't the most cost effective way to sell your show anyway. (If you are going to try to do television, investigate "spot cable" ads). You can't afford to buy televisions spots, but this doesn't mean you can't or won't be on television! You can probably afford some of the following:

Postcards
Posters (small and large – for windows, walls)
CDs
DVDs
Flyers
Websites
Email Campaigns
Youtube Videos
Stationary, Envelopes/Return Address Label
Your Press Kit

Which of the items above will be useful depends on your target audience and what you plan on doing to market your show. E.g. If you don't have a way or a place to put up a whole bunch of small posters (which go well in the windows of stores) then there is no reason to produce them. If your target market isn't younger, there's no reason to develop a place for prospective audience members to download ring tones of the music from your show.

You'll need to put together your marketing plan (which things you are going to do and when you are going to do them), but in the meantime you can start development of your press kit – which you'll need for multiple purposes, including getting "free" publicity or mentions in the press.

Your Press Kit

Your press kit is a collection of some of your marketing materials. You put everything into a nice folder and give it or send it to people who might help you promote your show. More on obtaining publicity later – but at this point realize you want to make your show look as professional as possible. That's why you need a press kit.

If you call up a radio station and say "help me promote my show", there is a small chance you'll be successful. If you call them up, say that, and then say "I'll send you our press kit", they will at least take a look at it – AND you will have a much better chance of getting some coverage. Just the fact that you HAVE a press kit puts you MUCH further along the path of getting people's attention. Then they are much more likely to realize you have a great show and they would be smart to cover it.

What Goes in Your Press Kit?

Your press kit can be as simple as a nice folder – which should be in your show's color scheme (!!!) – with a logo stuck to its cover. Sticking on a logo is as simple as running to an office supply store and buying some labels, such as Avery #8164. These are approximately 2.5 by 3.5 inch stickers. You go into

Microsoft word or some similar program, and download the template from the Avery website. (avery.com). Word actually has these templates already embedded in the software in some cases.

Put your logo and any information on each of the 6 sections of the document (you repeat the same thing six times). I recommend you include your website and phone number on the label. Then use a color printer to print out the document on a sheet of the labels. Peel off one of the labels and stick it on the front of the folder. That's the outside of your press kit.

Here's what can go in it:

- Press Release(s)
- Cover Letter
- Synopsis of Show
- Photos of actors or (better yet) from your show
- A link to where they can download the photos online
- How to Get Tickets Sheet
- Copies of any press you have already received
- Copies of any marketing material you have created (e.g. a couple of post cards)
- A business card (which has your show's logo, website, phone, contact name)
- A CD and/or DVD
- Song List
- Lyrics to a song or two
- Cast List & Bios
- Audience Quotes
- Anything else you think they might be interested in

You do not have to include everything listed above. You can also put it or not put in certain items (e.g. DVD) based on cost and whether you think the recipient needs the item.

"Fancy" press kits developed by major ad agencies often show up in magazine editor's mailboxes. These kits are often contained in some special packaging that is very expensive. That's fine for a multi-million dollar movie. You don't need it.

If your material is good they'll investigate it. Your show and what it is about is what should sell your show. The intriguing positioning and description (think "fearful passage of a death marked love") is what will reel them in. It's your show's benefits and "USP" that "sells" your show. You do not need expensive packaging. The fact that you put together a coordinated, good-looking press kit is enough.

Your Press Release

Your press kit should have at least one press release in it. That is a "current" release. You can also include copies of any past releases.

You can pay a publicity agency a lot of money to develop a press release for your show – or you can simply follow my example for you on the next two pages.

20 January 2009

World Premiere – New Musical "Sublet" to Debut at Theater 80 - St. Mark's on Valentine's Day

New York, New York (January 20, 2008) – Brian Teasley Presents, a Manhattan-based production company, announced today the debut of "Sublet", a new musical by Rodgers and Garfunkel on Valentine's Day, February 14th, 2008 at the Chanhassen Theater in New York City.

Incorporating the funky rock and roll music of numerous local musicians, "Sublet" is a romantic comedy musical about a couple that meets during a fight over an available apartment. The show leaves audiences literally dancing in the aisles.

"'Sublet' is a great date show", says Andrea Swanson, a New Yorker who saw a preview of the show. "The story is sweet and romantic, and the show girl dance numbers seemed to please the guy I was with".

"Sublet" stars an Actor's Equity cast, including Tom Anderson and Emily Gradder. It is directed by Steven Thompson, who is best known for his work on the show "Dogs". Music is by Eli Bolin. "Sublet" debuts on February 14th and runs daily at 8pm except Mondays. The location is the St. Mark's Theater, 80 St. Mark's Place in the East Village.

For tickets, please visit www.subletshow.com or call 1-800-GET-TIXX

Photos, videos, and additional information are available for download and use at: www.subletshow.com\press

Producers and stars of the show are available for interviews and on-air performances. Please contact for details.

About Brian Teasley Presents:

Brian Teasley Presents LLC . (www.brianteasleypresents.com) is an entertainment production company specializing in shows originating in New York City. Previous works include the revolutionary "(Insert famous show name here)" and the critically acclaimed "(Show that was cool and got good reviews but didn't sell any tickets)"

For Immediate Release Contact:
Brian Teasley
646.414.1100
www.brianteasleypresents.com
Email - brian "at" brianteasleypresents.com

© 2009 Brian Teasley

#####

All of the preceding information will fit on a standard 8.5 by 11 piece of paper. The "#####" is the symbol that notifies the recipient of the release that they have received all of the content.

Notice that for the most part the press release sticks only to the "facts" of the news, and does not embellish or try to "sell" the show. You tell them WHO is putting on the show, WHAT it is, WHEN it is, and WHERE it will be. If possible you also work in your description of the show and it's positioning.

You are allowed to embellish a bit – and the quote in the middle from an "audience member" does that. But if you talk about how fantastic the show is and your release ends up reading too much like a sales pitch, it will get ignored.

To create your press release, simply amend the example so it fits your show. You can and should create releases for other newsworthy events. Obviously you want to announce the opening of your show, but you could send out a release for your casting, your preview shows, your opening, your "special events", your "special guest stars", your new famous star who is taking over the lead role, how your show ties into "today's headlines", etc..

If you need more examples, suggestions, or tips, visit:

http://www.prweb.com/writing_release.php

That website has some great information about how to write a press release. They have suggestions on what to do and what not to do. But in general, the example I provide for you should be sufficient.

How to Receive Press Coverage

Now that you have a press release, a logo, and some other marketing materials (e.g. a synopsis of the show and bios of the cast, and maybe a list of songs) you have enough material to create/fill a small press kit.

So how do you get press coverage?   There are a few possibilities.

- You can hire a PR (public relations) agency to do the foot and phone work for you.
- You can send out your press release through a wire service.
- You can mail your press kit directly to contacts at media outlets.
- You can have members of the press hear about your show and contact you for information.
- You can run into them on the street and personally ask them to cover your show. I have run into a famous columnist in New York City on more than one occasion.

Always, always, ALWAYS have a card or postcard from your show on you AT ALL TIMES. Better still, have excerpts from your show on your iPod, video phone, PDA, etc. Then you can SHOW them a sample of your show. I've "sold" a show to somebody with 16 bars of music stored on a PDA I had with me when I met them. I didn't even explain the show – I just played the song, and all it took was 16 bars and they were sold.

You never know who you might run into. It can and will happen anywhere at any time. If you are prepared, then you will be able to take advantage of the opportunity.

Let's take a look at some of the "how to get press coverage" options.

PR Agency?

Due to the cost, you probably do not want to hire a PR agency.

The people who work at a good public relations firm are well connected. In part you are paying for their "rolodex" of phone numbers.

They know the right contact names at all major media outlets (TV, radio, newspapers, magazines, etc.) and with a phone call or two MIGHT be able to get coverage of your show. They are also usually VERY expensive.

I know one company that hired a PR firm to garner some publicity. The company paid the PR firm $15,000 per month as a "retainer". The company was actually not really ready to use the PR firm, so the PR firm just kept billing $15,000 per month and collected the money – and the PR firm DID NOT DO ANYTHING!!

My point is a PR firm will be happy to take your money. They will also not promise you any results, because they can not guaranty any results. So your money, time and efforts are better spent on other outlets.

On the other hand, if you have a friend in the PR business, ask them to help you. They have access to contacts, etc., and might be able to assist you at no cost.

This is another reason you need to have your press release and press kit ready-to-go FIRST. If you tell your friend, "Hey, I have a press kit and a press release ready to go – any chance you can help me get it in front of a few people?" they will be impressed that you have your act together. You have also made the process a lot easier, and it has a lot higher chance of being successful.

On the other hand, if you ask your PR friend to help you – and you do not have a release ready to go, and you do not have a press kit ready to go, you are asking them to do that work for you. They won't want to do that and are much less likely to want to help you.

Using a PR Wire Service

You can send out a press release over a wire by yourself. The two easiest choices are www.prweb.com and www.prnewswire.com . At the time of this writing, prweb.com costs you around $140 per press release. Prnewswire.com requires a registration fee and costs roughly $700 per press release.

Originally PRweb was a free service. You submitted your release and it went out to a list of people who had opted in to receive the press releases via email. The people who requested the emails DID include writers at major news organizations. Over time, more and more people found out about the free service, so the quantity of the press releases submitted increased and the quality and value of the topics decreased.

To combat this, prweb instituted fees for the service – and you now must pay for distribution of your release. Prnewswire has a higher cost, and this also reduces the release of "frivolous" news announcements. If something costs $1000 to publicize you are going to make sure it's a newsworthy event before you send out the release.

It's unfortunate that the services are expensive for small shows, but the cost weeds out many worthless press releases. This increases the chance that your release will be received and read.

There are different levels of service and distribution. Right now the option to include video with your release seems like a good deal – since few people are sending out video with their releases. This will change over time, of course.

When you send out your release, realize that some people will have set filters on their "receiving" capability. They want to receive news about certain topics. "Off-Broadway" might be a keyword for some. "Musical" and "New York" might be other required key words that some recipients want. "Chicago Theater" might be good keywords for other recipients.

This means that you want to stuff as many appropriate key words into your press release so that you reach as many people who are looking for your news as possible.

*If you use a PR news wire of some sort, **think about appropriate key words** and work them into your press release.*

See the "keyword tool" information in the "Google Adwords" section of this book for more key word ideas.

You submit your news to the PR wire service and indicate which categories of news into which your release fits. "Arts and Entertainment", "Music", "Theater" are all likely categories.

Sending Out Your Press Kit to the Press

You definitely will want to send out your press kit to anyone you think should cover your story. Certainly you'll send it to:

- Heads of the "Art and Entertainment" sections of all of your local newspapers
- Programs that cover theater or shows on any local radio stations. Note that you probably need to specify the name of the program and the host to increase the chances of your kit reaching them
- "New Local Music" shows on local radio stations (if your show has new music)
- The "listing" section for appropriate local magazines and newspapers (most publications dealing with entertainment have a weekly calendar of some sort – you want to be in it!)
- Contacts related to your show's participants. E.g. the hometown newspapers of each member of your show, plus anyone they might know in the media. You have an ensemble of people and you never know who might know someone who works at a publication or press agency. Get their contact information – and you or the cast member can send them a kit with a handwritten

note. Sure, nobody in Cleveland may come to see your show if is in New York, but if a cast member is from Cleveland and you get press coverage there, it sure looks good in your press kit.

Include a cover letter and tailor it to the recipient. E.g., most people would never think to try to market their musical via the "new music hour" on some FM radio station (even though once-upon-a-time America got many of its' hit songs from Broadway shows). However, I think it's a great idea. Why? Because program directors are looking for interesting programming, and they've already covered hundreds of local "up and coming" rock bands. So covering an "up and coming" rock *musical* is something different for them.

If you storm in with a truly new, fresh news story with good music, they might just give you a shot. "You mean you guys have a theater show with current, edgy popular music? Let's hear it!" will be their response. Radio stations love breaking new artists. It helps with their "cool" factor. They might even end up sponsoring your show. Not such a bad result from sending out a press kit, right?

My cover letter to such a radio show would include something along the lines of, "Hey, I know you guys don't usually cover musical theater shows in your "New Music Mondays" program, but we have a brand new show that is going to blow people away. I think your listeners might love our new songs. If you have a chance, please give us a listen at: myspace.com\subletshow" (And/or I'd include a CD in the kit.) Then the included press release would mention the cast is available for interviews, etc..

Don't think it could happen to you? I had a business with a news story that I thought would fit in well with a certain program on WOR radio in New York City. WOR is a powerhouse AM radio station based out of Manhattan. They are one of the original "clear channel" radio stations (as opposed to the corporation now known as "ClearChannel") which means you can hear their signal from a very far distance away, especially at night.

I put together a press kit in the exact manner described in this book. Two weeks later I was sitting discussing my idea with the host of one of the station's shows. It was that simple. I put together a nice press kit with a couple of press clippings and a post card, and a couple of press release examples. I included a short and sweet cover letter than listed two or three reasons why I though their audience would like to hear about the story. I sent it to the program, care of the radio station. They emailed me and we set up a time to meet. It can happen to you, too.

Since you already have a press kit, it won't take but a few minutes to call a radio station and ask them how to make a submission to a specific show. Alternatively you can ask for their guidance as to appropriate shows, but then you are asking them to do work for you – and that is always a bad idea. Do you think the person who answers the phone really wants to help you that much? So do a little research, and you'll be on the right track.

Who Do You Send it To?

So exactly who do you send your press kit to if you don't have a list of contact names? I don't know. Call up the publication and ask them. You might want to check their website first, as they might have the contact information listed there.

For example:
http://www.timeout.com/newyork/section/get-listed

Time Out is a weekly entertainment magazine in New York City (and other cities) that has a calendar of events. One or two lines in a magazine might not do much in terms of traffic to your show, but every little bit helps. Plus it's a combination of exposure to your show that drives people to see it – so every little reminder you can have is good.

When you call the publication or station, you simply call the main phone number and say something like, "Hello, I'm producing a cool new musical theater show and I'd love to send a press kit to the appropriate people at your publication/station. Can you tell me who that is, or transfer me to somebody who would know?" Call all your local publications, radio stations, and television stations and obtain the contact info. THEN look through the publications and find the names of people you think would be interested in your information.

For radio stations, listen to their shows and/or visit websites to determine appropriate shows for your content. Send a press kit to them as well as the people on your collected contact list.

Note:

- Major monthly magazines have deadlines about two or three months before the date that appears on the cover. So if you want your news covered in certain issues, you need to plan accordingly and get your news to them early
- Weekly publications usually need a week's advanced notice for listings
- Publications that will write a story based on your news need about two to three weeks advanced notice (maybe more, maybe less) to cover your story.
- Make sure you give them plenty of advanced notice or they will not be able to cover your show even if they want to

Note: **Do not send out your press release for the debut of your show (or anything else that is fairly close to the opening of your show)** *until you are ready to sell tickets.* If you are not ready to sell your product, do NOT waste the publicity. Wait until you are ready to go! Said another way, get your act together early. Figure out how you are going to sell tickets and get that set up early on.

If you have things set up early, you'll be able to take advantage of all of your publicity and sell as many tickets as possible. Don't be like the Kodak Corporation.

At some point in the 1990's there was a new "revolution" in photography - something about being able to take panoramic photos. The digital revolution was just about to hit like a tidal wave, but these guys were pushing this new "panoramic" photo capability.

The marketing and PR departments did a great job of garnering publicity. There were stories in many publications and they even had a front page story in the Wall Street Journal. Very, very good stuff.

Unfortunately nobody had checked with the manufacturing and distribution portions of the company. When the publicity hit the streets, there were NO CAMERAS available for purchase. They were not in any stores, anywhere. It was *six months* until the cameras hit the retail shelves! Highly amusing, unless you sell Kodak cameras.

When/How

Make sure you have enough advance notice for the publication when you send your kit to them. Make their life easy – do not put them on a deadline, because they won't work to it. Instead they'll through your stuff away.

Put your press kit folder inside a large envelope from your show. If you haven't printed your own envelopes at a print shop (there's no reason you need to), simply create a "return address label" and stick it on the center of the envelope. Use the Avery #8164 and put your logo and return address on the top half of the label. The bottom half is where you'll write or type in their address. Stick the label in the center of the envelope, insert your press kit (don't forget to include a tailored cover letter) and send it to them!

- Do not call them to see if they received it (except if you have an existing relationship with them, or some other extraordinary situation)
- You can follow up with a postcard a week or two later

Will You Get Publicity?
…or How I Got Mentioned on "Regis!"

If you send out a press release, will you receive coverage? Maybe. Maybe not. Here's a secret, though. Media outlets NEED your news. Without news, they wither. **The better your story, the better your chances of getting coverage**.

As an entrepreneur, I have many different areas of work. A few years back I started a "Data and Analysis for Marketing" service for ad agencies and other marketing groups (www.teasley.net for more information). I wanted to receive some publicity, so I thought about what special things I could come up with that might be "news worthy".

Since the business was (and still is) about data I figured it should have something to do with that. After thinking for a few days, I decided to take the U.S. Census Data and use it to come up with a list of "Top 10 Cities in Which to Find a Single, Rich Man".

I did the analysis, set up a bunch of related files on my website (top 10 list, a list of the ranking of all U.S. cities, biographic information, information about my services, etc.) and sent out a press release via prweb.com.

I waited a couple of days… and nothing happened. The release had been read by quite a few people on the service (they track that information) but there didn't seem to be any coverage. Then at the end of the third day I was driving home through a scenic portion of Connecticut after speaking at a conference. I checked my voice mail and there was a message from the New York Daily News. They wanted to ask me a couple of questions about my story.

The cell phone reception stunk (thanks, Sprint) so I couldn't get a connection to return the call until I returned back to my office. By then the folks at the Daily News had gone home. I figured I'd missed my chance, at least immediately – but I was wrong.

The next morning I was preparing to leave on a trip to Boston. The phone rang and it was KSFO radio in San Francisco. "Hey, we're calling about your 'Top 10' Rich Man story and we'd like to put you on the air in 15 minutes if we could", said the voice on the phone. "Ok, sure!", I answered. And 15 minutes later I was talking via AM radio to tens of thousands of people in the Bay Area in San Francisco.

We ended the segment and I hung up the phone. The phone rang. It was a production assistant from "The View" from ABC television. "We wanted to confirm a few things in regards to your story", he said. "Ok!" I replied. The guy mentioned the article in the Daily News.

After the call I figured I should see if I could find the article. So I ran down to my nearest newsstand and got a copy of the Daily News. I flipped through the pages trying to find the paragraph or two about my story. I couldn't find it.

Confused, I literally went back to the front page and said, "Ok, it's not on the front page". Then I turned the page to scan inside. "Ok, it's not on page two inside…" Page three had a picture of Gisele Bundchen wearing a snake, plus some other huge article. That certainly wasn't our couple of paragraphs. But then my subconscious said something to me, and I noticed my name on the page. It turned out that the ENTIRE page three of the New York Daily News (except for the photo of Gisele) was about my "Top 10 Places to Find a Rich Man".

That was crazy.

I went back to my office. I wanted to track press mentions, mainly to be able to use them for my own marketing purposes, so I emailed some colleagues and said, "Hey, if you happen to see mentions of this, please let me know". A couple of hours later one of them emailed me back. "You might not believe this, but you were just on Regis", he said.

Apparently to fill time – the media haa hours of air time they need to fill every day – some shows read from newspapers and comment on the stories. Well, my "story" was prominently placed in a major New York newspaper, so Regis Philbin read and commented about me and my survey.

I ended being interviewed by CNN Radio, some station in Texas, San Francisco, Wisconsin, and Pittsburgh – and a couple of others I don't remember. An Associated Press writer wrote a story about the list and put it on the AP wire. It ended up in about 100 newspapers across the country – and it was covered by numerous radio stations throughout the U.S..

My website traffic went through the roof. In a couple of days I probably had ten to twenty thousand visitors. I received a ton of press clippings. For about two weeks people I knew treated me very differently. Suddenly I was famous. I knew it was a "15 minute" type of thing, but it sure was strange. I even received a few strange multiple-page letters in the mail from women complaining that their city shouldn't be on the list because the men in their town are awful.

How much business did I receive from the publicity (this is a book about selling things, lest you think I forgot)? None – at least not directly. I did send out a couple of proposals, but I did not make any money directly off the publicity. However, the press clippings definitely help convince other prospects who have come along since then. Being in major news outlets does wonders for your credibility.

If I was going to do the same thing today, I'd do one thing slightly differently. I would have the full list of all U.S. cities and where they ranked available on my website, but behind a paypal button. You send me $4.99 or maybe $9.99 via paypal and you can then instantly download the list. It would be an easy way to make some spending money. And now that I'm thinking about it, maybe I'd add a "How to Pick Up Single Men" book or something like that. (Always think about how to sell more. More on that later)

Your "Take Away" Points from This Story

What are the important points of this story?

First I had a unique story. Admittedly it was a bit silly (I'm embarrassed to say it made the front page of a Pittsburgh paper, while a story about U.S. soldier's deaths was on page four). But certainly "Where to find single rich men", based on U.S. census data, is compelling to some people.

Second, I purposely released the story in February – and prior to Valentine's Day. January and February are traditionally slow news months. Something has to fill the airwaves and print space, so the media outlets need content. EVEN REGIS NEEDS CONTENT. So don't think your story won't get covered. If it is interesting to some people – and especially if it is "news", then it can get coverage.

I thought somebody would cover it will a Valentine's Day angle. But I struck out completely on that. Maybe I didn't release it early enough – or maybe that was just not quite the right idea. It doesn't matter – I missed completely on that part of the equation.

That's a very important piece of knowledge: Many things you will do in your marketing will not work the way you planned. They might not work at all, in terms of directly selling tickets. But some things you do will work. For many ideas you execute, you won't know which ones will work until you try.

Get a Gimmick/Story for Your Show

Ken Davenport is the producer of a show in New York City called "My First Time". He came up with a gimmick – anyone who is a virgin would be allowed into the premiere for free. He put out the word out, and the story was picked up by the

Associated Press. That means it gets covered all over the country. So, he found a unique marketing angle, and got a huge amount of publicity from the story.

So what can you do that ties into your show and is a worthy story? Is there some unique angle? Can you conduct a promotion with a local store, restaurant, etc. that might have something in common with your show? Is it an interesting historical piece? Does it play to something that happened on a certain date? If so, maybe you plan the show so it opens on that date – and the local paper will cover it as part of their coverage of that day.

For example, the Puerto Rican Day parade is a huge event in New York. If you had a show about Puerto Rico – or with Puerto Rican music – or with a celebrity from Puerto Rico, etc., you might just be able to obtain some coverage because of that.

Remember that the newspaper, magazine, radio, etc., people all have air time to fill. Give them something they can use. Make it as easy as possible for them to cover your story. Have photos, videos, mp3s, etc., ready for them on your website. Make it as simple as possible for them to cover your story.

Publicity "Stunts"

Almost anything you can do to attract attention to your show is a good thing. The ability to think of and pull off a unique publicity stunt is something that requires a creative mind.

The "My First Time" press release announcing that virgins would be let in free to the show is a great "stunt". I think the

"Top 10 Cities in Which to Find Single, Rich Men" story qualifies as a "stunt", too.

Bus and airline companies start new routes and announce that initial fares are $1. This receives press attention. Some Broadway shows sell tickets the first day for a dirt cheap price, tying the price to the name of the show if possible.

Trying to obtain public attention, some companies have set up tents outside their store so they can say "People are already in line, camping out, to buy this new product...".

If you have a show oriented to children, you could have a story telling hour at a local mall. Or have a character there that kids can get their pictures taken with (I assume by this point you know to make it so that the name of your show and/or website shows up in the photos some how). Maybe you should have a "face painting" booth. Think that's crazy? Talk to the folks at "Wicked" who do just that at street fairs.

As always, think about your target market and where they might see you. Think about the "media" (or medium) that is involved or best, whether it's print, radio, television, online, a street corner or other location.

What does that media need? What do they need a story about? What would they want to cover? What would work well on the street and get attention? What would the local paper cover? You have notified the local paper about the cool event that is going to happen on that date/time, haven't you? If they do not cover it, you can send them photos and a short story after the fact. You never know what they might cover. If it's fifteen minutes before deadline and they have one space in their newspaper to fill and you just sent them a cool photograph... in it goes.

Do Something Different

Do something different. Something. Anything. Figure it out and do it. **If you do something unique, you will get noticed**.

If you simply mimic everybody else's advertising, everybody else's approaches, everybody else's messages, everybody else's shows, then what are you telling your target audience? You are telling them you are just like everybody else! Why should they bother to come see your show if it is no different than any other?

The reason you are marketing your show, the reason you are advertising your show, the reason you are putting on your show **is** – (or at least should be) **because it is different than other shows**. If it's not, then there is no reason for anybody to come and see it. Your marketing needs to come from a position of "we have a unique offering" rather than from a "we need to sell tickets" perspective.

This applies to your press release and press kit efforts, but it also applies to your show and your marketing efforts overall. You can and need to come up with some unique ideas. They will greatly increase your chance of getting noticed and getting attention, both from the press and from individuals. That will help you **sell more tickets**.

Doing Press Interviews

If/when you are asked to do an interview with the press be smart about it. Practice ahead of time. Know what you want to say. Rehearse it.

What should you say? Well, you already know what your show is about – and you know your positioning statement. If you don't say those things during your interview, verbatim, then you failed.

Also – if you are "only" the producer or writer for a show – consider having one of the actors or performers conducting the interview. They might already have a lot more camera experience than you do. Cameras, lights, etc., are all very distracting and they take some getting used to. You'll start wondering where you should put your hands, turn your head, turn your body... how should you sit... what should you wear....

I sat next to a friend of mine as she did an in-audience skit with David Letterman. I sat through the afternoon rehearsal (with a stand in for Letterman) and then attended the taping of the show. Right before the segment, I was amazed how nervous I WAS – and I wasn't even going to be doing anything!

The fact that Letterman was about to come over, and the cameras were going to be on, really made me nervous. I'm embarrassed to admit it, but I'm also smart enough to know to have somebody with experience handle things they'll be better at than I will. She nailed the bit, and the show had a great segment because of it.

If you are personally going to do an important television appearance, start studying what goes on at other similar shows (or the one you will appear on) and mimic what works. Practice ahead of time. Rehearse.

If someone is going to do an interview or appearance for you, work with them to make sure you get your show description, positioning statement, and ticket selling information into their head.   When the host says, "Tell us a little bit about the show", that's your/their cue to parrot your description and positioning.

The Internet

The Internet is a tool you obviously can and should use to market your show and sell tickets to it. However, having a website about your show is of little value by itself. You have to drive people to it and use it in the correct manner.

Besides your show's website, there are also other aspects about internet marketing that will help you sell tickets. You should be involved in all of the following: a website for the show, myspace.com, facebook.com, ning.com, emailing, videos, show "commercials", videos of audience members raving about your show, samples of your music, monologues, etc..

Let's cover a bit about each of these.

Your Show's Website
The easiest way to save a lot of money in terms of developing your website is to mimic the website of a major show that's of the same type as yours. They've spent between fifty and a hundred thousand dollars developing their site – so why not just take what they decided on in terms of content and mimic it?

Spring Awakening was the first Broadway show to truly leverage the capabilities of the internet. At the time of writing, the home page of their site has a great high energy feel.. a mention of the eight Tony awards, and gives the user three easy-to-read options: Enter the Website, Buy Broadway Tickets, Buy Tour Tickets. So they FIRST thing they ask you to do, if you want to, is to buy tickets.

Since selling tickets is the NUMBER ONE reason you have a website, make it EASY for visitors to buy tickets from your website. If they have to hunt to figure out hot to buy tickets, your website is sub-par.

Spring Awakening has done a great job with their site. You can learn a lot from it. Steal whatever knowledge you can from it.

Meanwhile the "Altar Boyz" show has done a nice job of leveraging the web for encouraging fans of the show to share information with each other. There is a dedicated fan base for that show – and hopefully there will be for yours, too. Why sell somebody just one ticket when you can sell them five… or ten… or more.

The following items should all be included in your website if possible. They should each have their own page. Also if possible, these should be tabs or buttons/links across the top of your page. That's the best navigation system (as opposed to down the side of the page or across the bottom).

Check list for your website:

- Buy Ticket
- Description of Show
- See Photos and/or Videos
- See Press Reviews
- Buy T-shirts, CDs, etc

- Listen to Music Samples
- Theater Info, Map, Show Times
- Contact Show Info (customer service email, phone, press contact)
- Email Sign Up
- Cast Biographies and Photos
- Info & Photos for Press Use (if you put a paragraph for press use, somebody will use it verbatim in their story. That's good)
- Forum (via Ning.com or…)

So look around at "good" sites and steal whatever worthwhile ideas for content they have. However, you should strive to do something *different* – or you will just be doing what everybody else is doing.

If you can come up with additional uses of online tools and resources that other's have not thought of, then you will receive more attention.

If you have a historical play, links to videos and articles about the period of your play – or excerpts from historical biographies might be a way to go.

If your show is for kids, can you embed some type of online game to your site? Or sing-along music (especially if it is from your show). Maybe some sort of "follow-the-bouncing-ball" (or maybe some other animated object) that shows the words and goes in time to your music. You will need someone who is proficient programming or creating in "Flash" in order to make this work, but it is not too difficult.

Your website is important. But the single most important thing you can do with the internet is... Email

Email

Everybody has an email address that they use. Not everybody is on myspace. So if you announce a show on myspace not everybody will know about it. I have found shows after-the-fact that I would have attended had they just sent me an email about it. So you MUST use email as part of the marketing of your show.

Your website should definitely have a way for site visitors to sign up for news about your show – including updates on rehearsals, new casting, any media appearances you receive – and special ticket offers ("Only available to members of the (cool show name here) email list").

You have a couple of choices here. You can use a free service like yahoo mail or you can use a paid service that will give you a few more features, including "auto-responders".

Yahoo Mail (or Google mail, etc.)

If you are going to use yahoo mail or another free email service, I recommend you create a new email address that will only be used for show emails.

Once you create the account, you can load in the email addresses for the email recipients. You should (hopefully obviously) load the email addresses and other contact info into

76

the contact/address book – so you do not have to type in their email addresses every time you send out an email. You'll simply "check all" and you can send an email to everybody in your contact list.

You can also easily IMPORT contact names into the yahoo address book and then send emails to those imported people, too. Do you have ten people working in your show? If they aren't going to send out emails to their contacts (they should) you can ask them to send you a ".csv" version of their contact list. A "Comma Separated Value" (.csv) file is just a certain file format that makes it easy to exchange information between different computer programs.

To export (or import) a contact list as a csv file – go to http://address.mail.yahoo.com   Over on the upper right side of the page there is an "import/export" button.

If each of your ten show members sends you ten to twenty contacts, you can easily import them and you'll quickly have 100's of contacts.

Alternatively you can enter contacts one at a time. There's nothing wrong with this approach. Do the work – that contact list will come in handy.

More Email Addresses

Another way to obtain email addresses is to get a list of them from anywhere that might be possible. Do you have friends or colleagues that might have an email list of people who have attended their shows? Maybe there is another show running that will trade with you... there will let you use their list one time – if you in turn will promise to deliver email addresses of all the people that have attended your show.

OR.. maybe they can send out an email to their list – and advertise your show – and you do the same for them. The email they send out should have a link to your website – and then the people can sign up there to receive emails from you.

Again, they could also (or instead) export their list (probably to a .csv file_) and you can then email to it after importing it to your email contact list.

Paid Email Service

Yahoo, gmail, and hotmail are famous free email services. There are also paid email services that you can use.

Aweber.com is one that is fairly well known. They charge about $55 for three months of use. **Constantcontact.com** is another service that starts at $15/month.

One good thing about this approach is that you can use it and use an email address specifically from your show (goodinfo@yourshowname.com, for example) and when people receive the emails you send they will be from that email address (from your show) and not from a yahoo account. It will look a bit more professional with the "yourshowname.com" as part of your email address.

Another benefit of a paid email service is that they work to keep emails from their service off the spam filters and email blockers that are installed by various internet service providers.

They also allow you to see exactly who opened your emails and what they clicked on within the email. This can help you understand what people are most interested in.

You can also use aweber.com to send out an automatic series of emails, since the service provides you with "auto-respondent" capability.

For example, if you have a "click here to sign up for show info" button on your website (and you probably should) then when the person signs up for the emails they will immediately receive whatever "thank you" email you have programmed into the email stream. Then the next day – or two days later – or whatever you feel like is appropriate – you can automatically send them another email.

In one email you can automatically send some press reviews of your show. In another include some audience member comments. All those emails will be sent out using whatever you schedule you specify. You create the email "stream" and they are sent out automatically, starting with the "thank you" email and continuing from there.

The reason you do this is to remind them of your show. In the meantime you should occasionally send out "real" news about the show in separate "one off" emails.

Content of Emails

There are quite a few things you can email people about in terms of news about your show:

- First Rehearsal of YourShowName!
- One Week Until Show!
- Opening Night
- Press Review!
- Your Help Needed for YourShowName (Survey!)
- Ticket Specials
- Cast Member news related to your show
- Special Offer (email list members only!)
- New Music Clips on (website, myspace, etc.)

If you have people signed up for emails about your show, they are in a special category. They WANT to hear from you. Don't disappoint them by not emailing them – but also don't send them lame emails. "Don't forget about our show" is kind of a weak email. But inside information about your show is something they'll want to hear.

Why are these emails important? Because many of the people who have signed up voluntarily for your emails will tell other people about your show.   Treat these people nicely.   It's also possible that members of the press might hear about your show and be on the fence about attending or writing about it.   Your emails might just be the thing that prompts them to action – and they might just have signed up for your automatic email service and you didn't know they had done so.

Ning.com

Depending on how you look at it, Ning is either a service or a set of online tools that enable you to add a "user forum" or "social network" to your website. People join your "network" and can post videos, comments, see a calendar of events, etc., all about your show. It's free to use and simple to operate and use.

This site was developed by Marc Andreson, who is the technical guy who created Netscape, the original web browser. I happen to know Marc and the Ning CEO – and they have been developing the idea for this site since about 2002. It's now available for use – for free! Well, it's free if you let them post ads on your site. If you want to banish the ads they will charge you a monthly fee. For your show I recommend banishing the ads.

The service gives you the capability to develop your own online "forum" on any topic in you want. In this case you could use the service to develop a forum for your show. It is a very quick and easy way to start a "community" around your show.

You should encourage your cast members to join the forum and answer questions, post experiences they have had in regards to the show, etc.. Make sure they have been "prepped" in terms of your story description, positioning, and current marketing offers. You want everything to be as consistent as possible in terms of marketing your show. And make no mistake; actors talking to anyone about your show in any manner are marketing your show.

Myspace.com & Facebook.com

Different people use one or the other, some use both. You should have your show on both. You can post news, photos, videos, and people can sign up to receive news (blog posts) from you.

On myspace your "friends" will be notified any time you update your myspace "page". So if you add a new video, everybody will be automatically notified.

Keep your pages CURRENT! It is disheartening to go to a page and see it is obviously out-of-date. Who wants to go to a stale show that doesn't even update their myspace page? It doesn't matter if you main website is great to people who are only looking at your myspace page. If you do not use your myspace page much, then make sure IN BIG LETTERS it says people should visit your show's main webpage.

You should link as a "friend" to as many people as you can. While this strategy was originally used by some bands to get exposure to many people, the technique (which is free) is now being used by everyone – because it's free and they think it is how they will get worldwide exposure. The end result is that the friend thing has become in large part "spam", although a different flavor than the usual email spam.

The reason you SHOULD get as many friends as possible, especially links/connections with anyone even remotely affiliated with your show, is that friends of those people will find you. The "friends of friends" will have heard that their friend is involved with some interesting show (yours). When they see your bright and shiny logo (which should be your main selected photo) they will think "oh, that's the show she said she is involved in, let me check that out". Then they visit your page – and hear/see all the great info you've loaded in there… and you **sell more tickets**!

On a different myspace topic – if you have the capability of hiring an actor for your show that has 13 "friends" on myspace, versus signing up an equally talented actor that has 5,482 "friends" – which actor will likely help you sell more tickets? Should that influence casting decisions? Certainly. Producers hire famous actors to help sell tickets, shouldn't you do the same?

Blogging (and Google Alerts)

Let me be clear. I don't like "blogging". I don't like the word at all, and I hate the term "blogosphere" even more. For the most part, I think we've reached the stage where there actually are an infinite number of monkeys typing at keyboards.

BUT… there is a marketing secret involved with blogging, and you can use it to get your message in front of some people who you definitely want seeing your information.

Here's how it works at the moment. Let's say a local newspaper arts and entertainment writer is using the Google Alerts system (http://www.google.com/alerts) . This system alerts them (via email) to any new online web pages that contain whatever keywords they are monitoring.

For example they might be in Chicago and monitoring "Chicago" and "Opera", since they want to know anything about the opera world that is occurring in Chicago. Let's further say that your show is a small opera show and you will be putting it on in Chicago. Or the tour you are taking your show on runs through Chicago.

You don't have a way to get your press release to them directly (and be certain they received it) since you do not know their email address or even who they are. However, there are two ways that might get your press release (and any other information) to them.

One method is directly via a press release service. This can get your release to them if they have signed up directly with the service. However, your release also will get to them via a few web pages that will be automatically created that will contain your press release. The key words "Chicago" and "opera" need to be in your release. If so, the Google alert system they signed up for will automatically notify them about the web pages that were automatically created containing your press release.

The other method is to create a "blog" page. You can use blogspot.com or blogger.com and post a few "blog entries" (ok, enough with the stupid word "blog") and the Google Alerts system will find your pages – and will automatically send an email to the critic in Chicago with a link to your page!

Every couple of days you update your... online "diary", and Google finds the page and sends along notifications to anyone who has requested alerts about key words that are contained in your new posting. Using this method your "keyword recipients" will receive your message every time you update your "blog". Just make sure your new entries contain the appropriate key words.

Once the above sinks in, you'll eventually realize you should start "stacking the deck" of your press releases and postings to include key words that are relevant to your show. A bit more on that is in the Google Adwords section of this book.

By the way, there's no reason you shouldn't use Google Alerts to monitor news about your show. If you receive press or website coverage, or someone makes a blog post about it, there's a good chance Google will pick it up and email you an alert.

Google Adwords

There are two uses for you of the Google Adwords program (http://adwords.google.com). The obvious one is to buy key words so that your show is advertised, via the little ads that get put up on the right side of the page when someone searches on Google on the key words you have purchased.

The second reason to use the Adwords program is that you can use the google "keyword tool" to find out what OTHER key words are searched upon when people are doing searches similar to the terms in which you are already interested.

Buying the keywords and placing the ads is a simple process. You can literally log on and have an ad campaign running in about fifteen minutes if you want. I suggest you first do a little more research because it will save you money. But if you wanted to you could easily get a campaign up and running from scratch very quickly. The good news is you only "pay per click" – which means it costs nothing to set up your campaign. You only pay your pre-agreed-to fee each time somebody clicks on your ad.

If other advertisers want your key words, then the price per click will go up like in an auction. Pricing varies. It used to cost as little as $0.02 per click, but Google decided to deviate from their "Do no evil" maxim and push you to pay $0.10 per click, at a minimum. Popular key words cost much more.

Which Key Words for Your Show?

You should purchase the name of your show as a key word or phrase. If it is an unusual name, you can purchase likely misspellings of the word(s) so people will still see your ad even if they don't type in the correct spelling of the name of your show.

However, you probably do not want your ad for your show "Cats" being displayed every time someone includes the word "cats" in a search, so maybe you purchase the phrase "cats musical" or "cats theater" (and while we are at it, "cats theatre" since some people will spell it that way).

If your show is called "Puerto Rican Pride" and is about Puerto Rican Independence, then you should purchase "Puerto Rican Pride" and other related phrases such as "Puerto Rican Play' and/or "Puerto Rican Independence Play". Some people might hear about your show as the "play about Puerto Rican independence" and do a search for that and not your exact title.

The key word tool will show you OTHER words or phrases that you might want to purchase. E.g. if you use the tool to search for other words like "Puerto Rican Independence Play", the key words tool might suggest "Porto Rico Independence play". It might suggest "Hispanic Play New York" (if people know about your Hispanic play and know it's in New York, they might enter that into Google when looking for information about your show).

If you really want to learn about Adwords (it's useful for many businesses, not just marketing shows) visit: http://www.perrymarshall.com/

Tickets

If you don't yet know about Brown Paper Tickets, you should check them out at www.brownpapertickets.com. They are set up to handle online ticket sales for your event. They are also set up to deliver "hard" printed tickets for your event.

Through their "API" (automated programming interface, for those of you that haven't lived in Silicon Valley) you can hook up your show's website to their service and sell tickets directly from your website.

The cost is $1 per ticket plus 2.5% of the ticket price, or $0.10 per hard ticket. This can be added on to the ticket price or you can absorb it if you wish.

The hard tickets have a perforation, so you guests will go home with a ticket stub in their pocket. That stub will have the name of your show and the website listed on it – along with anything else you want printed on it.

They will even let you upload a diagram/map of your theater and then you can sell tickets with assigned seating within a section. You have to tell them the ranking of the sections in terms of best-to-worst seats in the house, and they use that to sell the tickets.

With real-time inventory capability you'll know exactly what's going on with your show in terms of ticket sales at all times.

General Advertising (Newspapers, Magazines, Direct Mail, Postcards)

Wouldn't it be great if you had a large advertisement about your show in every newspaper and magazine in town? Maybe. If you had a large budget, and ran the ad for consecutive issues, you would sell some tickets that way. But... it probably wouldn't be cost effective for you (the cost of the ads could outweigh the ticket revenue generated). It's also very expensive. If you are running a small show, then you probably won't have enough revenue to cover the ad expense anyway.

Rack Rates & Other Costs

If you want to investigate "traditional" advertising media anyway, you can visit the websites of television and radio stations and find their "advertising media kit". You can also call them up and ask them to send one to you if you can't find the information online.

The kit will contain information about pricing, deadlines for submissions, and technical information about the ads themselves (sizes of print ads, or formats for audio files for radio commercials).

The actual price paid for advertisements is always lower than the "rack rates" contained in the media kits. 20% off is guaranteed to be taken off just for the asking. You can get up to 50% off, especially if you are willing to take "remnant space". This means your ¼ page ad will be run whenever they have unsold space – and on whatever page the space is located. It very well might end up being "prime" space. It's a lot like the "half-price" tickets to Broadway shows sold at the TKTS booth in Times Square. Sometimes you'll receive "remnant" space in the last couple of rows for your price range. Other times you can receive "house seats" – and end up sitting in the best seats in the theater.

How to get cheap ad space? Call up the publication's ad sales representatives. Tell them your situation, how you have a great show – and then put on a touch of a sob story. Tell them you'd love to place an ad but you are small and have virtually no money. You'd like to send them a press kit and then discuss if there's anything you can do to get some dirt cheap ad space. Maybe their other clients would like a few free tickets? (Editorial people and writers are usually not supposed to accept free gifts, but sales guys are a different story. They'll bend whatever rules they want to in order to make people happy (and, ahem, make their monthly self-imposed ad sales quotas)).

FYI – the Time Out New York Media Kit can easily be found on their website (http://www.timeout.com/newyork/). It has information about print ads, online ads, and email ads.

Other tidbits:

- The smallest ad space you can purchase on the NYC subway is one "box" (I'm not sure of the correct term – it's about the size of a portrait painting – roughly 3 feet high by 2 feet across). If you run one box in $1/10^{th}$ of all the cars, the cost is approximately $10,000 per month

- A small ad in a publication such as a tourist magazine in New York City runs about $800 per week.

- Print publications like to price by "CPM". This is the cost of your ad per each 1,000 people that (supposedly) receive the publication. So to figure out the true cost of your ad, you have to know the circulation of the publication – or ask them specifically to tell you what the cost of an ad is, rather than the "CPM".

- TV ads are expensive, but radio ads might be cost effective, depending on the size and scope of your show. The good news is that you might be able to produce your own ad on the cheap, since you are in a creative field – and radio stations accept mp3 files as a format for commercials. If you are in a smaller town with a small local station, call them up and ask them what can be worked out. You never know what might happen. They might sell you cheap ad space AND let you do an on-air appearance, since they need to fill air time! Be prepared to send them a press kit, of course.

Post Cards

Most likely you'll want a post card for your show. It should contain all the "basic" information about your show – and most importantly information about HOW TO BUY TICKETS. Your website should be featured prominently. You will not have much real estate to work with, but a lot of good information can be conveyed economically if you give it some thought.

If you are good with Photoshop, you can produce the card yourself. Then you simply send your files to a print shop and they will manufacture the cards for you. If you aren't good with Photoshop (or other similar program) then have a "creative" person (a.k.a. "graphic designer") design the card and produce the file for you.

The technical specifications for a post card can be found at http://www.4over4.com . These guys produce zillions of postcards *every day*. They are high quality cards and used by many, many small shows in New York. They also will ship your cards to you anywhere in the U.S. (Load your files via their website, have your cards in a few days, anywhere in the U.S.) You might save a little bit by going elsewhere (although their prices are good), but you will not receive as good quality cards as you will from these guys.

A 4x6 postcard is the "standard" size. If you are placing your cards in card racks made for such purposes (often found at clubs/cabarets) this is the normal size. But there is no reason to not go smaller to save money, or larger if you fell there is some reason to do so.

The funny thing about postcards is that I don't think I have ever seen one actually mailed in the postal service. They can be used:

- In Press Kits
- As a handout on the street (street teams)
- Handed to people when they come in to see your show, preview, reading, etc.
- Given to every show member to hand out to their friends
- Given to every show member to hand out to ANYONE they meet

The last item in the list above is one of my pet peeves. I've talked with many performers in New York City... and countless times they have told me about a show they are about to be in. I've said, "Sounds great, can you give me a card or info about the show?" I'm ready to take a card from them and I'll probably then remember to get a ticket for the show. The answer is always, "Oh, no, I don't have one with me..."

A warning to anybody who works on one of my shows: If you are a member of one of my shows and I see you on the street and you do NOT have cards about my show with you, you will be in trouble. If you are trying to sell tickets, then EVERYBODY involved with your show is a potential ticket seller. At a minimum they should have show information with them in the form of a card. They could easily also have tickets with them to sell on the spot. Why not? Especially if it is a general admission show!

Direct Mail

You should consider conducting some type of direct mail campaign, where you send an envelope or a postcard to recipients, for your show.

If you send an envelope, realize you can put more than one piece of paper in an envelope for the same postage cost. You can get three regular pieces of 8 ½ by 11 paper in a standard business envelope for the regular first class stamp rate.

To get cheaper postage rates you will need to prove to the post office that your mailing list is up-to-date. This means it has to have been run through the national change of address (NCOA) process and the addresses have been standardized. If a list broker sells you a list, ask them if they have taken these steps (NCOA has to be done every six months, and a certificate has to be issued).

Then the mail has to be sorted in the "carrier route order" or zip code order. This is the order in which the carrier will deliver the mail. If you have that information, that's actually easy to do in Microsoft excel. Talk to someone at your local post office and check out http://www.usps.com   I really dislike the US post office, but they are able to deliver mail. Unfortunately FedEx is not allowed to deliver to your mailbox.

The technical information above is given only for those that might be trying to do larger mailings on their own.

When people sign up for your email list, you can also have them enter their mailing address information. Those people can then receive your direct mailings.

How to Cut Your Postage Cost

If you are sending an envelope, consider cutting your postage costs by sharing expenses with a co-mailer. Is there another show or area restaurant that might want to include something in your mailing? Maybe you could include a "After the show, use this coupon for $5.00 off dinner at Fred's Diner, located down the street from the theater".

Call up the restaurant owner. Tell him what you are up to. Go meet him. Show him your press kit, which will impress him and show him you are serious (that's another reason we started this book out by talking about the press kit). Tell him how much it will cost to be in your mailer, which will go out to... however many people.

If you are daring, see if you can stick him with the entire cost of the mailer – or at least more than his share of the costs. You are doing a lot of extra work anyway, so why shouldn't he pay for the work you are doing for him. Tell him you'll mention him in the program for the show – and/or you'll have your after parties at his restaurant. Be creative.

Time Tested Mailing Facts

I have spent a lot of time analyzing direct mail results for some major companies. Inevitably, the response rates to the mailing are influenced by three things, in this order: list, offer, creative.

List: You can send the coolest, best designed letter in the world with a great offer, but if you send it to the wrong people you won't sell any tickets. So how do you get a list of people that might attend your show? Talk with theater owners, club owners, record store owners, promoters – anyone who might share your same target audience.

Offer: The immediate impact of a direct mail piece with an "Order now and receive ½ price tickets" will likely be a sales rate higher than "Order today and you'll receive 10% off on tickets". So you will sell more tickets with the half-off offer, but probably not enough to make up for the loss of revenue.

Creative: The "look and feel" of you mailing can impact response rates, although it is not as important as the list. The mailing should be consistent with the positioning, color scheme, fonts, feeling, etc., of your show.

This same thinking applies online. What sites you are on and who you send emails to is more important, followed by your marketing message, offer, and creative look. Again, you could have the coolest banner ad in the world, but if it shows up on the AARP website for retired people and you have a rock show – the results will not be good. Where you are and who sees your marketing is the most important aspect of your efforts. This doesn't mean the other things aren't important, of course.

"Down & Dirty" Marketing

I think there term "Guerilla" has lost its meaning when related to marketing. Let's call this "alternative" or "doesn't-cost-anything but time", or maybe "Down & Dirty" marketing.

Here are some ideas for low cost marketing. Some will fit well with your show and some won't. It' depends on what your show is and what your target market is. If you have a Rock and Roll music show, standing outside of a show like "Spring Awakening" and handing out flyers makes sense. Standing outside of "Phantom of the Opera" and doing the same thing does not. If you have a rock and roll show your target market is more prevalent at "Spring Awakening". Your target is also much more prevalent at a rock club.

So remind yourself who is your target market, and figure out where they will be. Then conduct any of the following to them, as appropriate.

- **Leverage Prior Shows at the Same Venue**
You can hand out cards outside your venue a week or two before your show. That's obvious, but not too many shows do it. A more effective effort would be to ask one (or two or three) of the shows the weeks prior to your show if you could do one song, or skit, or piece from your show at some point during or before their show. Offer that they can do

the same, you can get them into your show for free, you'll exchange email lists (don't forget to ask if you can do a one-time mailing to their list), etc.. Then when you do the "special preview" make sure you have other people from your show there with cards, information, wearing t-shirts with your shows name on it, etc.. Again, that's why you develop marketing material ahead of time

-   Do Previews at Other Venues
If you are doing previews or staged readings or full rehearsals that are open to the public, conduct those showings at venues other than the one you will be at for your actual performances. Choose a theater with a good mailing list, and make sure they'll help you sell a few tickets to your staged reading/preview shows by listing you in their regular marketing efforts, including their emails. This way you'll get word of your show to people who go to shows – and a completely different list from the one your regular venue has.

-   Street Fairs & Art Fairs
Does your town have street fairs or art fairs that need performances? Figure out when the events are and get scheduled to perform the month & weeks prior to your show - and during your run, as possible. These events need entertainment, and if you send them a solid press kit and a good demo CD (or video if you don't have music) they will book you. Just like the press, the have time to fill. Make their job easy and fill some of it for them. Do this as early as possible before they've booked all the slots.

- **Neighborhood Canvassing**
Are there local restaurants that will let you put small "table top" post cards in small 4x6 picture frame displays and put them on their tables or checkout counter? Maybe for a nice ad in your program they will. Show them your press kit, tell them what you'd like to do. Make sure they realize it's no cost to them. Recommend they include a "$5 off" coupon in their program mention (or "bring in your ticket stub for...").

Are there stores that will let you put up a display by their checkout counter? How about a sign/poster in their window? People love to help "up and coming" talent. They love to be associated with the arts. Maybe they want a free ticket to your sneak preview show (and you want all the local merchants to come see your show so that they all can talk about it to their customers, so if they come to your show they are actually doing you a favor!).

- **Sneak Preview Show or Special Offer for Previews**
Figure out who the key "word of mouth" people are in your area. Who are the "influencers" of your target market? Get those people to your show with a one-time only special sneak preview for "Local VIPs" only. DO charge them money to see the show. But if you are going to sell tickets for $20, make the VIP preview tickets $5 or $10. Give them a great deal, but don't make it free. Your show is better than free. People will like the show more if they pay something for it. It inherently has more value, and they have to justify that for which they paid money. They will see more value in your show if they have to pay for it. Make this a special EARLY preview. You can let VIPs in to future shows at your discretion, but these are people you

want at your show early. You can "position" the special preview as a VIP thing you are doing for "in the know" people only.

- **Joint Marketing**

This has already mentioned, but can you market your show in tandem with some other entity? Is there another venue, establishment, or organization that needs some publicity by being associated with your show? Does the local "Puerto Rican Pride" organization need an event to promote and bring their members to? Did a new local establishment open and they need to ingratiate themselves to the neighborhood? What better way than supporting and helping a local show?

- **Charities**

Is there a logical charity that would want to be associated with your show? Does a character in your show have a disease? Contact the Heart Association, the Lung Association, etc.. Maybe they'll put you on their monthly calendar that goes out to all their supporters. Maybe they'll raffle off tickets to your show at their next auction. Maybe they'll let you perform a segment of your show at their next charity luncheon. Maybe they'll buy a block of tickets if you make a special night – and have one of their members speak during or after your show. Maybe you can give them tickets and it'll be a tax deduction. Maybe you can sell autographed copies of programs – or sell autographed versions of your DVDs or posters... at the end of your show in an auction format, donating the money to the charity. Maybe you'll remember to ask them about all of these things in the meeting you set up with them after you call them and ask them if it makes sense to meet.

Ongoing Efforts

Your marketing efforts do not end when your show opens. Not by a long shot. Assuming you are going more than one performance (and potentially even if you ARE just doing one performance) there are many things you should consider doing as part of your efforts to sell more tickets.

The most important thing you can do to sell tickets is have a great show. More on that in a little bit. But there are also other tactics you can use to sell more tickets.

Nightly Photos

As people are waiting in line (which you can make them do if you are so inclined) you can set up a "Red Carpet" area with a back drop with the name of your show all over it (or better yet, your website address). Have someone take photos of your guests, just like at some big event. Then announce that the photos will be put up on the website and they can download them from there. You can let them download the images for free, which hopefully they will email to all of their friends. And/or you can use a service like shutterfly.com or showmeproofs.com and you can sell prints to them and make a few $ for the efforts. I suggest giving away the digital downloads for free.

Selling Photos with Characters

While many performers love hitting the stage, they don't realize many audience members want to be up there, too. So why not sell them the opportunity to walk up on stage and get their picture taken with the main character? You can email them the photo – and Photoshop it to contain your web address, etc.. Backstage tours are big hits, too. Some people spend BIG bucks to go backstage at a Broadway show. They see it as a thrill; you use it as an opportunity to market your show.

Nightly/Weekly Prize Drawing

Have everyone fill out their name, address, and email address and put it into a fishbowl. Send out an "And the winner is…" email the next day and then ship them a free t-shirt or CD. You can ask them which prize they would like on the piece of paper they submit (which you give to them). This lets them choose – AND gives you survey information about what your most popular selling merchandise is.

Hand out a "Please Help Us!" Sheet

As people are walking out (or stuffed into your program) hand them a card or small sheet of paper that says "How you can help us!" You can also stuff this paper into your programs. Tell them step-by-step what you want them to do. E.g. "Please email all your friends tonight or tomorrow and send them the address for our website. Don't forget if you had your photo taken you can pick it up there tomorrow." Also mention sending postcards, which are mentioned below.

Hand Out Postcards for Actual Mailing

Have someone saying "Free postcards to mail to your friends" as the audience members are walking out the door. You can print a special version of your cards that have a check box on them that say "I liked the show", "I loved the show", "Don't miss this show", etc.. They simply sign it and address it and send it to their friends.

Street Teams

You can hand out information and even sell tickets with a street team. Exactly where you should place your team depends on your target market and the location of your show. Think about who might be able to come to your show and determine when the most populated time is at that location. Lunchtime near office buildings? Major walkways after work? Night time near "restaurant row"? Many people are out looking for things to do. A good person on the street will be able to sell tickets and help them see your great show.

Hand out Cards After a Separate Performance

I have two contrasting stories to illustrate this point. One is a good story, one is a bad story.

Good Job Story: One of the characters in a show I saw recently was the "Green Fairy". You may know this character from the movie "Moulin Rouge" – or you may know her association with the drink Absinthe. The part was a small one, but the audience loved her. As audience members were leaving after the show, outside on the walkway they were surprised by the Green Fairy! There she was, still bouncing around in character, and happily greeting each set of guests. She was handing out cards to HER OWN personal show – and not the show the folks had just seen. Everybody loved her, and I saw many people reading the cards she was handing to them. I am sure she sold some tickets to her show in those few minutes after the other performance. It was a fantastic bit of marketing!

Bad Job Story: I went to a music showcase. I really liked one set of performers – all of whom do their individual gigs in addition to the group songs they did. After the show were they handing out cards about their gigs to everyone who walked out, like the Green Fairy? Did they hand out a piece of paper that said "If you liked my music, you can hear more here: www.(namehere).com or come see my upcoming show at..."? Did they do anything to further market themselves or sell tickets to any upcoming shows? No. When I actually went looking for any of them to find out information about any upcoming gigs (so I could see if they would fit into some show ideas I have) I saw them walking out the door. They were leaving at least one customer (me) and possibly others.

Other Shows

Cut deals with other current shows. They let you use their show/audience to market your show, you'll do the same for theirs. If you have more things in place (and you will, if you do most of what's in this book) you'll do a better job than they will. Perform before their show. Perform at intermission. Hand out cards in the street after the show like the Green Fairy. If you hear about a major show that is closing, maybe they'll sell you their list of attendees.

Pricing Your Show

Set the prices for your show in such a manner that you get as many people into the venue for the first few shows. Word-of-mouth advertising is very critical to the success of your show, so you want to get people in to those first shows so they will help you with sales for future shows.

You can have a "regular" preview night, and sell tickets at a discount. You may need a press/media night at which you recommend press members attend. I'm of the mindset that you should still charge them something for their tickets. If you charge for the tickets, the people will be MUCH more likely to show up, even if the charge is nominal.

You can have a VIP "locals only" preview night, where only people with local driver's license IDs can attend at a special price. Or maybe only local business owners attend... and maybe there is a social event before or after your show. Think about your show and what makes sense and is congruent with how you have positioned your show.

Once you reach critical mass with word-of-mouth advertising, then you can phase out the discounts. This should be a part of your ongoing marketing strategy. You'll likely need to offer discounts on other hard-to-fill seats occasions, and consider raising seat prices on weekends – when demand is higher.

Also know that some people will always pay for "premium" goods and services. About ten to twenty percent of people always will buy the highest priced goods when offered a selection. So consider having a "gold package" that includes good seats, autographed photos, t-shirts, a quick backstage tour, whatever might be appealing. Those are things that cost you nothing extra, and you can sell them as a premium package at a premium price.

There is also a set of people who do not care if the tickets cost $19 or $29 (or $20 vs. $29.99). The extra ten dollars makes no difference to them. That is another reason to sell seats at different costs, as long as you differentiate the service or product that goes along with that extra $10. Maybe the extra $10 seats are reserved, or don't have to wait in line to get in, or…

The premium/enhanced/increased pricing doesn't have anything to do with "Selling More Tickets", but it will affect your revenue. You can use the extra money to print more postcards or do that costly email blast, and that will sell more tickets.

Books, CDs, DVDs, T-shirts

One other aspect that people often think of as revenue streams (which they can be) that are additionally part of the marketing equation is that of books, CDs and DVDs. You need as many of these things as you think you can break even on in terms of sales income versus cost. You can even lose a little money on these items – since they are actually marketing materials for your show.

If somebody plays your CD in their car, or sets the program from your show on their coffee table and their friends respond to it, you've just gotten the message about your show to new potential customers. If they flip through a cool book or program that features great enticing photos from your show, you are on your way to selling tickets to them.

So put together a few things and make sure their covers feature your show's name and/or logo and/or website address. Make it large so somebody can read it from across the room. The more exposure your show receives the better.

T-Shirts

Especially at the outset of your show, consider selling t-shirts at or near cost. How much would you pay to have somebody wear the name of your show on their shirt for you all day? The more exposure your show receives the better.

The Show Itself

If you do everything in this book and have a great show, you will be in great position to **sell more tickets** to your performances.

Many of the cast members of "Spring Awakening" report it was word-of-mouth "advertising" that saved their show. They had a decent marketing plan. They received some good reviews. But the audience numbers were still questionable. There were empty seats. Tickets at the "Half-Price Ticket Booth" (aka TKTS) were easy to come by. The show played to houses that were not full.

But then slowly the empty seats began to disappear. Word was getting out about the show. The ad campaigns, as strong as they were, were out there – but it took people to see the show and tell their friends and colleagues to really sell tickets.

The show went on to win multiple Tony awards – and after that you couldn't get a ticket.

You need word-of-mouth "advertising" about your show to be successful. There are things you can do to make it easy for your audience to others about your show, but they won't help you unless your show is good.

Make sure it is.

"Brand Experience" &
"Show Experience"

Branding

The real value of "Brand" advertising is two-fold. One is make you as the viewer familiar with the name, logo, and product(s) in the advertising. The other is to transfer the feelings you have associated with the brand to whatever it is that the advertisement is associating with that brand.

Michael Jackson (remember him?) was paid somewhere between $5 million and $10 million for endorsing Pepsi cola. Pepsi was buying the associations people had with Michael Jackson (who was king of the pop music world at the time) and branding them into people's brains in association with their cola product.

If you have seen the brand/logo many times, it becomes familiar to you. The more familiar something is, the more you "trust" it. In regards to a show, once you are familiar with a show you are much more likely to buy a ticket to it. That's why you want consistency in your marketing materials and you want people to see the name of your show and its' logo.

It's a bit tricky to transfer your show's brand to anything else, since you might only have one show. If you are a production company you might consider "branding" your show with your production company's logo. Then in the future if you run another show or set of shows, you can "transfer" your production company's brand image to the new show.

Hollywood movies do that in a sense every time they say, "From the folks who brought you 'There's Something About Mary'…" Bill Graham Presents did a great job of this out in San Francisco when he was promoting the Grateful Dead, and Bowery Presents is doing a good job of making a name for themselves and transferring their brand equity (the value people put into a show just because it is put on by them) to the new bands they promote.

So there is a difference between branding a show and having a "brand" as a production company. That's a little more than I want to get into any further in this book, but it needed to be mentioned for clarification.

You need to focus more on selling tickets to your show and the show "experience" more than you need to focus on "branding" efforts.

The Branding & Show "Experience"

Marketers like to talk about the "brand experience" – which means they are thinking about your customer's total experience. This does not only mean "how did they like the show?"

A customer's experience with your show starts from the moment they first "interact" with your brand/show in any manner. This could be the first time they see an ad, the first time they hear anything about it, or a number of other occurrences. The experience with your show continues through the purchasing of tickets, continues through the moment they enter the theater, through the show, and continues AFTER the show.

If you really want to maximize sales of tickets to your show, you have to consider and try to cover the marketing opportunities that occur at every stage of that process. Since word-of-mouth advertising is very important to your show, you want to **make sure you do everything possible to make sure your audience members love their "Show Experience"**.

The Actual Show Experience

I recently went to a show that was in an area where there was more than one event going on. I couldn't find the correct location for the show I wanted to see, despite asking people who worked on the premises.

Why hadn't the person in charge of selling tickets walked around and told everybody about this specific show and where it was being held? Why wasn't there a large sign with the show's logo on it, helping me find where to go? I had actually walked right past the show's location three times....

That experience had a negative impact on me in regards to the show and the performers involved. The show also started late. Very late. Five minutes late? No problem. More than thirty minutes late? At least make an announcement as to what is going on. But that, not surprisingly, didn't happen either.

The show itself was very good. But do I want to recommend to my friends that they go see the show – when it might start an hour late, they might not be able to find it, etc.? Notice I'm not giving you the name of the show in this book. The performers could use the publicity, but they didn't make the grade in terms of something I want my reputation to be involved with. Had they just taken care of these things, they would get a free mention in this book – and maybe additional publicity and word-of-mouth advertising from other's who were in attendance that night.

More Show Experience

There are many things you can do to improve your guest's "show experience". These simple things WILL have an affect on your word-of-mouth ticket sales.

I'll skip some basic items, like making sure music is playing when they people come into the venue (if appropriate) … making sure it is not too hot or too cold in the venue, etc.. Those things go to the management of the venue and the actual content of the show.

Branding at Your Show – Getting Your Name Out

But what about "branding" at your show? How can you get the name of the show further into your audience member's brains? Is the name of the show on the ticket? Is the website address on the ticket? How about on the program?

The ticket and program might get thrown away by some people at the show, but it is also taken home by many others. Then those items lay on a dresser or table or counter... and are reminders of the great time the people had at your show. That keeps your show in their "Top of Mind" – and the more they remember your show the more likely it is that they'll refer other people to your show.

If you are in a band and you are playing at bars and other venues, think about your audience. Many people might be there that do NOT know anything about you. Your friends and "groupies" know who you are, but anyone who just happens to wander into one of your sets has no clue who you are.

The ONLY way they find out who you are is if you tell them. Announcing the name of your band at the end of your set, as in "Thanks guys we are (Insert Band Name) check out our CDs", works for anyone who is listening at that precise moment. But what about the others who came, liked you, but left?

Once upon a time there was an unknown band playing in Hamburg, Germany. On their bass drum, in large letters it said, "The Beatles". Anyone who came in would immediately know the name of the band.

Maybe your drummer doesn't want to paint the name of your band on his drum. But shouldn't you at least have a large banner made and hang it behind you? Or project the name of your band using an LCD projector?

Isn't that something you can do that will help you **sell more tickets**?

More "At Show" Branding

Some people will be brought to your show and they won't even know the name of it. Is the staff of the show, especially ushers and ticket takers, wearing something that indicates the name of your show? Do your guests immediately get into the "look and feel" of your show from these people? Does the staff help differentiate *your* show from every-other-not-well-marketed show?

When the audience walks in, do they see a gigantic logo from your show to let them know they have "arrived" at the show? Is something else going on to satisfy the needs of their attention should they need something? Music? A video? A "thank you for coming" message to read?

All of those things can help "Brand" your show, image, etc., into people's brains. That is exactly what repetitive advertising is all about, so why not do as much of it as you can while people are attending your event?

Drilling the name of your show into potential customer's head will help you **sell more tickets**.

Putting it all Together

There's an old joke about why the signs outside a "Go-Go" bar (is there such a thing these days?) say "Girls! Girls! Girls!". It's theorized that the conversation inside a guy's head goes something like this:

Sign: Girls!

    Guy: Huh?

Sign: Girls!

    Guy: Girls?

Sign: Girls!

    Guy: Girls!!!

Advertising people talk about ad "impressions". This is the number of time you actually see a certain ad. The "magic number" of exposures to a television ad so that you'll remember it – at the least cost to the advertiser – is supposedly three.

If you see an ad only one time, it won't drive you to do anything. Studies supposedly show that three is the number of ad impressions required to have the optimal bang-for-the-buck, so to speak. The guys who make the signs at the go-go clubs apparently knew this long ago, without the aid of a costly study from an advertising company.

This is precisely the reason why, at least in part, that if you watch television for some set period of time you'll see the same advertisement multiple times. They are trying to drill their product into your head.

What does this have to do with your show? Most likely you aren't going to be running television ads. But if you have read through this book you now know you have multiple "channels", or ways, to reach your target audience. In order to sell tickets to your shows, you MUST reach your target audience multiple times with your message about your show.

One piece of advice for marketing a show is that if you are going to do only one thing, then do not even bother doing that one thing. The time you spend going it will be close to worthless. You need to do many things. You need:

- Email
- Website(s)
- Press Coverage
- Music Samples
- Video Samples
- Show Descriptions and "Selling" Points
- Press Releases and Kits
- Postcards
- Lists (email, direct mail)

In order to optimize your marketing efforts, and to **sell the most number of tickets**, you need to coordinate your marketing efforts. You need to get as close to "Girls! Girls! Girls!" as you can, given your marketing efforts.

It does not do you much good if you send out a press release and get a press mention if the rest of your marketing materials are not in place. It does not do you much good if a radio station plays your song, but your website isn't ready – or it doesn't have a link to the ticket purchasing page. It doesn't sell many tickets if somebody walks down the street with the logo for your show on it – if the people who see it do not know what the logo is about.

If you do any of these things without the support of the others, in effect you have only one "Girls!" The response of the viewer is therefore going to be, "Huh?" That won't sell any tickets.

Your Marketing Plan

Your **marketing plan** is simply a document or listing of all the things you plan on doing in your marketing – and a calendar of when you are planning on doing them. Since some of these things are contingent upon previous steps, you will have to work backwards from the opening of your show, or a preview of your show, etc., to make sure you give yourself enough time to complete all of the steps in your marketing plan.

So let's work backwards starting with the Opening Night of a show. We will list steps we want to take as part of our marketing of the show and selling of tickets, and that way we can "back into" a start date that is required for our efforts.

Basic Marketing Calendar/Planning
Sublet
Version 030808

June 1st	Opening Night
May 23-30 shirts!)	Street Team Hands Out Postcards (wearing
May 23-30	Radio/Press Interviews/Press Mentions
May 18	Thank You for Coming Emails & Photos Uploaded
May 16, 17	Show Previews & "Locals Only" Show. "Help Us!" sheet & post cards to friends handout
May 10	Send Out "Opening Night" Press Kits
May 2	Initiate Google Adwords Campaign
May 1	Send Out "Previews" & "Locals Only" Press release to appropriate media outlets
May 1	Initiate Local Merchant Poster Program
April 30	Website Needs to Be Ready to Go

April 30	Need Postcards and Press Kits Ready
April 23	Final Week of Tweaking Website
April 20	Send Postcards to Printer (last date possible!)
April 20	Load Material to Myspace, facebook, ning
April 15	Send Posters for Merchants to Printers
April 14	Write Press release(s), Collect Biographies, song lists, etc. for press kit
April 13	Design Postcards
April 1	Website Work Begun in Earnest
April 1	Design Posters
March 30	Get Material to Website Designer (music, photos, site "layout" & content needs, description of show, creative brief, color scheme finalized, etc.)
March 15	Graphic Designer Works on "look and feel", logo, etc.
March 1	Work on Show Descriptions, Color Scheme Thoughts

So a very **basic** set of marketing efforts requires that you start your marketing efforts at least **three months prior** to the opening of your show. Notice that this schedule does not even have email streams built into it.

If you want to add press releases for castings and other "pre-opening" events, then the calendar needs to be extended a bit.

The calendar above is also not "padded" at all. If this calendar was being executed inside an advertising agency it would require more than three months to complete all of the steps. It's good not to be involved with large entities; you can get things done much faster than they can.

Note: It's important that you share your overall marketing plan with everyone that is involved with it in any manner. At least two things will come from this – everyone will see that their portion of work is only part of a much larger picture.

This means that everyone else is counting on them to hold up their portion of the work. Secondly, inevitably somebody will come up with a synergistic idea, where you can combine the marketing going on in one channel (e.g. on your website) with another (e.g. street team flyers).

E.g. Your street team can take photos of people passing by (children with a character photos?) and post them on your website. They passerby people can pick up their photos by going to the website.

If you have struck a chord with the press and you receive some coverage, you have the potential of any of the following happening to your potential customers:

- Radio Hearing (interview, mention, music)
- Printed Press Mention (article, website mention)
- Postcard from Friend
- Street Team Handed out Postcard to Them
- Email from Friend about show
- Email from Friend about their photo from show
- Sees Sign in Merchant Window or similar
- Friend Tells them about show

The more of these that hit your target audience the better, of course. But even if only TWO things happen to someone, the fact that they see information about your show twice greatly increases the chance that they will buy a ticket to your show. This is how you will **sell more tickets** to your shows.

I'll mention the billboards in Times Square again. If you had one there, it probably wouldn't sell tickets to your show by itself. But a billboard in conjunction with many other marketing efforts will have an impact and help you sell tickets, due to the multiple exposures that your target audience receives.

Exit Music

When you realize you have to start working at least three months ahead of time to market your show so you can sell more tickets to it, you may realize why many people do not sell as many tickets to their shows as they could.

However, with some work and coordinated effort, you can devise and execute an advertising/marketing/PR/ticket selling campaign that will probably be better for your show than one designed by an advertising company.

The more work you do on developing your campaign, the more tickets you will sell. Every action you take that is mentioned in this book will put you a step above and beyond other shows and other events that are competing for the public's attention. Every step you take takes you a little higher – and the higher you go the less competition there is.

The multiple exposures required to spur somebody into buying tickets to your show can be achieved. Obviously you need more than one marketing vehicle to achieve the multiple exposures, and this book shows you many options that are available to you.

Marketing and selling is also an ongoing process – one that builds upon itself in more than one way. The "multiple exposure" requirement is one aspect, but word-of-mouth also builds. One person tells a few friends and a couple of them come to your show. Then they each tell more friends, and that helps build momentum for your show.

You also are building audiences for your NEXT shows. If you do a good job keeping track of your current audiences, you will have a built in audience for your next set of shows. Repeat the processes in this book and the number of people attending your shows will increase.

All you have to do is to take the initiative and go through the steps outlined in this book. If you develop, plan and execute a multi-faceted campaign for your show you will reap the benefits of your efforts. You will SELL MORE TICKETS to your shows.

Now, on with your show.

Resources

Email

Aweber.com

Approximately $50 per quarter. Includes auto-responders.
Allow you to have multiple lists – so you could have "gold",
"VIP", "student" emails... or email lists corresponding to
different shows

Constantcontact.com

Templates you can use, good reporting and tracking. Roughly
$15 to $50 per month (depending on number of email
addresses). Also has survey capabilities – but charges for the
surveys. Free 60 day trial.

Surveys

Zoomerang.com

The basic service is free. You can ask up to 30 questions and
can obtain responses from up to 100 people. Good for getting

a basic concept of feedback from your customers and audience members

Surveymonkey.com

Similar service to zoomerang. Only 10 questions allowed in the basic (Free) service. Also ties in directly with "Mailchimp" which has email templates and will assist you with emailing your surveys

PR/News Wire Services

Prweb.com

Rates vary, but range from approximately $80 to $200 per release. No fee to join. Can and has resulted in major publicity in the past.

Prnewswire.com

Costs in the hundreds of dollars to join and then each press release costs hundreds. However, this service is used/monitored regularly by a higher level of media outlets.

Tickets

Brownpapertickets.com

These guys are trying to put ticketmaster out of business. That won't happen, but there is certain a need for such a service at a price that is reasonable. It will still cost you about $1.50 per ticket – and that adds up. On the other hand, that is less than $3 or more that other services tack on a ticketing fee.

Printing

4over4.com

A highly dependable, completely online based printing service that can be used by anyone, anywhere in the United States. They have a great system with very fast turn-around times. Their "4 over 4" color postcards have 4 colors on the front and back and are high quality cards. If you want one less thing to worry about, use these guys as your printer

"Social" Internet

Ning.com

A self-proclaimed "Social Networking" site. Will allow you to start an online "community" on any topic.

Orkut.com

Google's entry into "social networking". As of this writing, catching on on the west coast of the U.S. Not yet on track on the east coast.

Blogging

Blogspot.com, blogger.com

Two free services which you can use to create an online weblog. See segment in "Internet" chapter on how to tie this into Google Adwords

Selling Photos

Shutterfly.com, Showmeproofs.com

Upload photos, link to them from your website, sell them to your customers.

Sound

Matt Crawford – mattcrawford.net

This guy is a sound wizard. He's an even better drummer. If you have any type of sound project, from recording (live or studio) through editing and mixing, he is who you want doing your work. And if you are in the New York City area and need a drummer, he is one of the best.

Other

Google Adwords – Adwords.google.com

Google's easy-to-use advertising program which you can also use as a research tool. Use to purchase online ads for your show

Google Alerts - Google.com/alerts

Free system that will email you news about key words of your choice. Use to track online mentions of your show

Books

"Guide to Producing Plays and Musicals", The Commercial Theater Institute.

A relatively new book with sections from many different top Broadway producers and their associates. Includes a few sections on advertising and marketing of major shows, including examples of advertisements. A good behind-the-scenes look at putting together and marketing a show

"Influence: The Psychology of Persuasion", Robert Cialdini

If you need some understanding of the psychology behind what motivates and influences people's decisions, this well known book will give you some insights and examples. Good for understanding the "benefits" and description of your show

"Sex Money Kiss", Gene Simmons

At first I laughed when somebody suggested this book as a good business book. But then you realize – Kiss (one of the most successful rock and roll bands of all time) was and is masterful at selling themselves. Simmons is the leader of the band, and was behind most of their marketing ploys – including their famous make-up. There story fits well with many topics in this book. They had a unique product. They used merchandising in part as a marketing vehicle.

Simmons was smart enough to realize the name of the band needed to be displayed in LARGE letters at every show – which is why it always says "KISS" in their unique font, right behind the band - always. That unique font used to display their name became their logo, which they have used to brand apparel, lunch boxes, action figures, etc.. It's a great marketing/selling tickets story.

"Think and Grow Rich", Napolean Hill
If you have bigger plans than "just" selling tickets to a few shows, then this may be the book you need. It will show you the steps to take to come up with the new ideas and plans you need (that's the "Think" portion of the title) to do anything you want to do.

About the Author

Author, speaker, marketer and promoter Brian Teasley has spent over fifteen years in top ad agencies and Fortune 50 businesses, helping them improve their marketing campaigns.

He has analyzed parts of the Space Shuttle, flown a 747, and was deemed a (good) "witch" by the chief of a remote African village.

His writings and tools are used all over the world.

For additional information, speaking information, tour dates, etc., please visit:

www.teasley.net

www.ingramcontent.com/pod-product-compliance
Lightning Source LLC
Chambersburg PA
CBHW051541170526
45165CB00002B/828